the GREAT GIFT of TEARS

edited by Heather Hodgson

Edited by Heather Hodgson.
Cover design by Kate Kokotailo.
Book design by Duncan Campbell.
Cover painting, "Homage to the Mothers," 2000, by Dennis Bruce.
Printed and bound in Canada at Marc Veilleux Imprimeur Inc.

National Library of Canada Cataloguing in Publication

The great gift of tears

ISBN 1-55050-192-5

1. Canadian drama (English)—Indian authors.* 2. Canadian drama (English)—21st century.* I. Hodgson, Heather, 1957-
PS8235.I6G73 2002 C812'.6'080897 C2001-911306-4
PR9194.5.I5G73 2002C8 T33 2002

1 2 3 4 5 6 7 8 9 10

401-2206 Dewdney Ave.
Regina, Saskatchewan
Canada S4R 1H3

available in Canada and the US from:
Fitzhenry & Whiteside
195 Allstate Parkway
Markham, Ontario
Canada L3R 4T8

The publisher gratefully acknowledges the financial assistance of the Saskatchewan Arts Board, the Canada Council for the Arts, the Government of Canada through the Book Publishing Industry Development Program (BPIDP), the Government of Saskatchewan, through the Cultural Industries Development Fund, and the City of Regina Arts Commission, for its publishing program.

table of contents

This anthology is dedicated to my beloved mother,
Cree Elder C.W. ("Willy") Hodgson,
RPN, CSW, SOM, CM, poet.

The Storied Stage

The four plays in this anthology were written by three Saskatchewan Native playwrights – Floyd Favel, Deanne Kasokeo and Bruce Sinclair – whose artistic preoccupations have developed in a world very different than that of our First Nation ancestors. Their shared cultural task, each in their different ways, has been to recover and reforge aboriginal traditional spiritual resources for a space that is relatively new to Native people – the theatre.

The predominant cultural expression that predates our time and which comprises the ground for present and future artistic endeavours among First Nation peoples, is the *story*. *Story* has been paramount in our cultures because it has transmitted safely – through countless generations – the living gifts of our culture, language and history. Today *story* is still at the heart of who we are and it continues to play a role in virtually all of our gatherings, rituals and ceremonies.

The form of the story, which is multidimensional, is particularly important to how First Nation peoples pass on knowledge, as it is designed to harness and discipline young minds and fire the imagination. In that regard, characters and events in our stories are vividly portrayed, often moving back and forth through time, and through other seemingly endless layers of plot and character that exist both in human time and in a time when people and animals still talked to each other.

Important to the telling of our stories are our First Nation languages. My mother, a fluent Cree speaker, has long attempted to describe to me how vivid the Cree language is and how each word and phrase paints pictures in the mind. Cree words contain the excitement that seems to be built into their very utterance and in that animated sense, are equivalent to watching a movie. In fact, stories told by First Nation storytellers are not merely spoken, but rather, are performed. And the best storytellers give the liveliest performances because they rely not only on their voices, but on their entire being to tell their story. Eye contact, facial expressions, hand and arm gestures, are crucial to an effective telling of one of our old stories. With this theatrical picture in our minds, we are now ready for the stage....

Favel, Kasokeo and Sinclair are playwrights whose work is rooted in the tradition of the performed story. As a result, their plays contain many different but related stories – about individuals, about groups of people and their history, about animals and the earth, and about the myths and prophecies of old. While their plays have been written in a world that has become increasingly compartmentalized and segregated, they are playwrights who have not forgotten that art has no boundaries. In that spirit, their stories – retrieved and reshaped for the stage – have slipped into a new genre as easily as an animal might slip under a fence. These playwrights have taken the old stories and reshaped them for a new genre. As a result, our culture can express itself differently, for a different time, and for very different audiences. Our stories have found a new home *in the theatre!*

The character of the audiences now listening to our stories is very different than it was in the past. Audience today is crucial to the cultural dialogue, and although our stories have moved from hearth to stage, they still trigger emotional catharsis, but on a much larger scale. They also continue to express solidarity and empathetically identify with the sufferer. This – even if it does not create community – engages and often nourishes an audience, and also makes it conscious of itself as witness. So in this way, the plays of Favel, Kasokeo and Sinclair, bring very important voices to the processes of cultural renewal, self-understanding and historical critique. All of these playwrights pay their respects to the dead, converse with their ancestors – both human and animal – and then act on injustice through the writing of their plays. They retrieve our cultural inheritance, and share with us those gifts of value and knowledge that tell us who we are.

The plays herein are for a wide audience, indeed, and in that respect might be regarded as resources for cultural mediation – despite the sounding of a frequent pessimistic lament. And as Art, they are an extremely powerful medium through which transcultural understanding might begin.

The lead play in this anthology – *Governor of the Dew: a memorial to nostalgia and love* – is by Floyd Favel, one of the most gifted playwrights in the province today. Favel continues to break trail in theatre here, all across the country, and overseas. On the surface, *Governor of the Dew* is a tragic and gripping love story, but a close reading unearths an historical layer which deeply resonates with First Nation people. *Governor of the Dew* is *Quintessential Story* in the tradition of the finest of our First Nation storytellers. It opens with Favel himself as the frame narrator, moves back and forth through successive generations and many other stories, and then ultimately returns to Favel, to close. This is the story that stages the dramatic first encounter between Indigenous and European peoples; it is the story that will affect First Nation peoples until the end of time. It is the story of that historical moment, which Favel has given powerful and moving particularity.

All My Relatives, which was Favel's first effort as a playwright, is also informed by the old stories and myths. They are woven together against the backdrop of the long and uneasy shift First Nation peoples were forced to make from the bush to the reserve and from the reserve to the city. Despite its contemporary setting, every scene of *All My Relatives* contains stories about the *wîhtikow,* the prophecy of buffalo woman, the grandmothers, and the sacred, ancient belief in the importance of remembering. The painful transition experienced by the characters, who move from a starkly rich rural lifestyle to a flashy urban lifestyle, reminds us of the attendant division of loyalties and heart-wrenching dilemmas First Nation families, their children and elderly have to face when they must leave everything they know behind.

Deanne Kasokeo's adaptation of *Antigone* vividly illustrates the relevance of Sophocles' classic for First Nation communities in the grip of issues brought about through power and corruption. With biting clarity, *Antigone* shows us how an imposed political structure can contaminate the old style of band governance by corrupting a chief and council. In stark relief to the corruption is Antigone's morality, her unwavering allegiance to the practices of her ancestors, her respect for the rituals of the dead, her humility in the face of the spirit world, and her loyalty to family and community.

Mary of Patuanak, by Bruce Sinclair, is the fourth and appropriately final play in this anthology, and takes place on the eve of the virgin birth. On the surface the play tells the story about Mary – a university student who, like other First Nation students lost in the labyrinth of non-native academia, is alone and adrift. Separated from her culture at a very early age, Mary is linguistically and culturally alienated from her Dene roots, and it is on this level that *Mary of Patuanak* mirrors the experience known to many First Nation students today. On another level, no one will fail to be amused by the humour and irony in Sinclair's play, as it is a thinly disguised adaptation of the virgin birth. In a hilarious twisting of the facts, we witness a research journey of the Magi taken by three fact-hungry academics. So, while the subject matter of the play – cultural alienation, pregnancy, the pitfalls of a white education – is serious indeed, the characters and events provide light and often amusing insight into somber and dark experiences.

The four plays in this anthology have been read and discussed in manuscript form by students of English at the Saskatchewan Indian Federated College. In some cases, students acted out portions of the plays in class and the results were remarkable – all involved found the plays to be familiar and engaging. In all of these respects, the plays are powerful tools for literary and cultural instruction, so we are grateful to the playwrights. The settings, symbols, plots, characters and themes resonate with First Nation cultural significance to provide a perspective that has scarcely been available to students of First Nation or Métis ancestry, not to speak of the usual theatre-going crowd.

The plays in this anthology are part of the tradition whereby the wisdom of our ancestors is continuously adapted to the needs of new audiences. In that regard, the plays of Floyd Favel and Deanne Kasokeo, both of the Poundmaker First Nation, and Bruce Sinclair, of the Waterhen First Nation, are firmly rooted in the past while being relevant to the present.

– Heather Hodgson

GOVERNOR of the DEW:

a memorial to nostalgia and love

Floyd Favel

This play is dedicated to my late mother, Lily Favel, for her love of stories and words.

characters

NARRATOR

MOTHER

ROSE BILLY,
an old woman who is also the granddaughter of the Old Beaver

OLD BEAVER

Old Beaver as a YOUNG BEAVER

YOUNG WOMAN

Governor of the Dew was workshopped by the Takwakin Performance Laboratory and the Montreal Playwrights Workshop in October 1997. It was premiered by the Globe Theatre in October 1999, performed by Andrea Menard, and presented by the Globe Theatre and the National Arts Centre in Ottawa in September 2002, performed by Monique Mojica.

Act 1

NARRATOR:
This story goes something like this.
It's been so long since I heard it.
It's from another time, another place,
before I became a man
in this whorehouse of the world.

Back then we lived on the reserve,
beside the creek bordered by shadowed paths carpeted
with decaying birch and poplar leaves
and the soft footfalls at twilight of long dead ancestors.

There my mother would walk in the light
between dreaming and waking
checking her rabbit snares,
the morning broken by the sharp crack of ice
breaking with cold.

nimâmâ, nikâwiy,
your smile brightened the world.

I have only faded photographs
to evoke your memory
and your words, your stories.

This is a story my mother told me.

MOTHER:
Once upon a time, an old woman,
Rose Billy, was at home
one still summer afternoon
when all we hear
is the wind rushing through the leaves.

Rose:
Grandmother's Song

(chant)

niya ôma nôcikwêsiw
Rose Billy *kâ-isiyihkâsot.*
ôta niwîkin,
ê-pêyakowân,
ê-kaskêyihtamân,
êkwa mîna ê-kitimâkisiyân.
êkwa mîna ê-kitimâkisiyân.

(musical interlude)

niya ôma nôcikwêsiw
Rose Billy *kâ-isiyihkâsot.*
ôta niwîkin,
ê-pêyakowân,
ê-kaskêyihtamân.
êkwa mîna ê-kitimâkisiyân.
êkwa mîna ê-kitimâkisiyân.

(chant)

Rose:
I was at home.
I hear these steps on the porch. *mah!*
And a scratching sound on the door.
awîna êtikwê?
Could it be my grandson
who has gone away to school?
Or an old sweetheart
coming to warm these old bones?

So I open the door,
and standing there
is this old beaver.

wahwâ, 'toni nimâmaskâcihon.
ê-mamâhtâwahk.

hâm mosôm, tawâw!

MOTHER:
The beaver entered,
and sat beside the table.
The room was silent.
The beaver hung his head
and tears poured down his face.
His body heaved with his broken heart.

BEAVER:
I have lived my life in shame
and please, *nôsisê,* don't judge me.

ROSE:
mosôm, you know as well as I
that it is not us who can judge.

BEAVER:
tâpwê, nôsisê, kitâpwân,
kimiyo-pîkiskwân.
You speak truthfully and with kindness
which I do not deserve.

ROSE:
I gave him some tea, lifted it to his mouth
and he drank.
I wiped the tears from his eyes
and caressed his head.

hâm, âcimo!

BEAVER:
aya nôsisim, this story happened over there at the shallows
where the wagons used to cross.
This story is about the time I fell in love.
Yes, I was in love once.
To look at me, you would find that hard to believe, *cî?*

Rose:
No, *mosôm,* you are still handsome.
Your visit blesses me!

Beaver:
Yes, I was in love once.
It is difficult to speak about it.

hâm nôsisim, give me some more tea.

Young Beaver:
One morning, I was up earlier than usual
and I sat on the bank of the creek.
I looked at the red willows and poplars that lined the banks,
and listened to the birds rousing us to wakefulness and vigilance.

This is my home, *nitaskiy ôma!*
Someday, I will be the Governor of my tribe,
and this is our land.
I lifted my hand like this, and turned a half circle this way.
Then I lifted the other hand, and turned in the opposite direction
and said a little prayer,
wishing for long life and the health of our tribe
and for the unborn who come crying over the next horizon.
How naïve our prayers can be.
We never know what life will bring in the next hour,
and these events show the naivety
and ignorance of our understanding.

mâka, I believed in my prayers.
Was that not enough?
Yes. If I have been blessed in this life,
at least knew the taste of Faith,
however brief. Praise the Creator!

I went on my stomach and slid down the black mud slide
and splashed in the cool clear water,
frightening a school of jackfish ahead of me.

MOTHER:
He made his way downwards to the narrows
where the shade is cool
and where members of his tribe gather
in the heat of the brief summer,
to philosophize and settle tribal disputes.

Here the horses came to drink at dawn,
silently, warily, like outlaws.
They were led by the dappled stallion
who stood off to the side, keeping watch,
nose testing the air for signs of humanity.
New to this land,
they had been accepted by the various animal Nations
and given their space and freedom.

A distant solitude seems to be in their nature.
Perhaps it was memories of their past suffering
in the far south and across the Big Water
that have made it difficult for them to trust.

Here they found Peace.
Is it not true that
Peace is what we all seek?

YOUNG BEAVER:
I emerged and I saw some humans on the shore.
Their party consisted of a dozen horses
dark with sweat, and laden with trade goods.
Slowly and silently I surveyed this party.
The bearded men laughed and called to each other
in a language that I had never heard before.
wahwâ, 'toni ê-miyohtâkosicik.
One man sat in the shade
playing a musical instrument he held under his chin.
The instrument made a high beautiful sound
that I felt in the core of my being.

I drifted closer, seduced and curious.

And then I saw her,

this young woman
sitting on a rock by the creek.
How strange, her skin so smooth and bronzed,
her hair so long, black and wavy.

WOMAN: *(singing)*
Regretter

Regretter c'est combattre le temps
et tout au fond des entrailles
un chant d'oiseau à midi.
Si tu pouvais goûter mon coeur,
tu reconnaîtrais le goût
de la cruelle nostalgie,
la solitude de la grand-maman,
de la mûre fraîche de l'été,
de l'amant et de l'aimée.
Ton nom remue d'inconsolables désirs
dans ta sombre forêt,
sous un flou soleil d'hiver
chevaux venant s'abreuver à láube
dans l'ombre de la clairière
le lieu où les guerriers prient.
La solitude de grand-maman,
de la mûre fraîche de l'été,
de l'amant et de l'aimée.
Si tu pouvais goûter mon coeur
tu reconnaîtrais le goût
de la cruelle nostalgie.

(end music)

BEAVER*:*
Her eyes found mine.
The inadequacy of my condition assailed me
and I was never so aware of myself.
I knew shame.

I returned her gaze,
in spite of my shame.

What else could I do when faced with such a human?
Nothing in all my life had prepared me for this meeting.
Could she love me?

What would my tribe say if I brought her home with me?

namôya konita mâna kêhtê-ayak k-êtwêcik
ê-âyimahk ôma pimâtisiwin!
ê-papâ-môskotêhêyahk;
pôni-mâtoyahk;
êkosi ê-pôni-pimâtisiyahk;
nikiskêyihtên êwako!

kikitimâkisinaw nôsisê.

There I stood.
I was afraid, wondering if she will take me.
âstam, kinôhtê-pê-wîcêwin?
ê-nitawêyihtamân ka-pê-wîcêwiyan.

She came; she waded into the water
against the cries of her countrymen.
I reached out my hand.
The roar of the thundersticks was loud in my ears,
the smell of gunpowder harsh to my nose.
The thud of their bullets around my body furthered my resolve.
There was no turning back and I abandoned my body to Death.
Nothing lasts forever!

I took her hand
and swung her to my back.
Hold on tight! Hold on! Hold on tight!
And we dove.

Her people will have a great story to tell about me!
We swam along the rocks
at the bottom of the river.
We met some of my relatives
who were scurrying for safety
from the sounds of War.

We came bursting into the sunlight
with a huge gasp for air.
She was weak and collapsed in my arms.
She was even more beautiful.

Mother:
They say we came from the land of the Sun,
there someplace, where the land, sky and water meet.
It is there where it all began.
This is where the Muskrat had brought up land
from the depths of the water.
The little piece of Earth was clutched in his hands
as he emerged dead from his efforts.
From this we learn that
all earthly actions are accomplished with a sacrifice.

kistêsinaw, our Elder Brother, the Son of the Creator,
was floating on a raft, destroyed by Grief.
He delicately opened the hand of the Muskrat
and retrieved the little piece of earth
that had cost the Muskrat his life.
He placed the Earth into his hands,
blowing upon it all the while.

The land began to grow and grow,
and soon it made a little island,
then a larger island, *ôma ministik,*
until the land became as grand as we now know it.

Young Beaver:
niwîkimâkan, my love, mon amour.
ôtê ôma kâ-wîkiyân.
ôta ôma kâ-kî-pê-ohpikiyân.
ôta kîsta ka-wîkin.
This is where you will live also.

Act II

Mother:

Someplace far away, in the Land of the Twilight,
there is a vast plain.
A cool wind constantly sweeps this land;
in the centre, there is a Tree,
a Tree of Souls.

These souls rest on the branches
and make the sound of birds.
The souls closer to the top of the tree
are those whose destiny is to be great.

At the top is a nest and
in this nest, the souls we call prophets sleep,
those souls that come into our lives
and transform us, and our Religions.

Beaver:

nôsisim, you have no idea of the joy
that came when I brought her home with me.
Nobody had ever felt the pain of foreign love
as I did then.

Nobody.

Surely the Heavens saw fit to bless me that day.
This was yet another honour that was being bestowed upon me.
I, who was soon to be the Governor.

It is only the very few who receive the honour from the Heavens.
It is an honour which transforms the spirit.

Such a fool I have been.

It's hard to imagine my former greatness
as I sit here at your feet,
seeming to be begging for mercy and pity.

nôsisê, forgive me for burdening you like this,
I have come only to open the door of my heart;
ê-pâstâhoyân, I am paying for my sins.

ROSE:
mosôm, I pity you.
It is a great blessing you have given by coming to me.
niya, a lonely old woman who has lost her husband
and whose children have grown up and moved to the city.
I am grateful.
It is me who sits in front of you seeming to ask for mercy.

BEAVER:
Thank you, *nôsisê.*

MOTHER:
Tears flowed from Rose Billy's eyes as she sat
face to face with the old beaver.
She laid a pack of tobacco at his feet,
refilled his tea, and presented the tea to his mouth
as to an infant, or an invalid.
The drink soothed his soul somewhat,
and he sat quietly for a few minutes.

She went to the next room,
returned,
and laid colored ribbons next to the tobacco,
for she knew how to treat visitors
such as this old beaver.
With ribbons, tobacco, and tears.
Tears, the greatest gift of all.

YOUNG BEAVER:
We stood on a hill overlooking our valley.
You humans think that our lodges are dark and damp, but it is not so.

The arc of our lodge is the arc of our sky.
The floor of our lodge is the soil of our earth,
the walls are the horizons of our sky.

Here everything is plentiful and rich,
fish, berries, willows and poplars,
and all manner of nations share our lodge
and have their place, like they do in your world.

Our lodges were strung out along the river valley.
Our young swam playfully in the streams,
the adults were in the forest, preparing for the winter
which we could feel in the crispness of the dawn.

We made our way slowly to my village.

A great cry arose from the villagers
when they saw me and the stranger,
and all rushed out to look closer.
I introduced her to my people
and said that now, she and I would be husband and wife.

That night there was a feast,
and I told the story of how I faced the foreigners' guns
and escaped with my wife on my back.
There was singing and dancing
and I danced my joy to the light of the moon.

(dance)

There was only one pair of eyes which mattered to me
and it was the eyes of my wife.
Her face shone ghostly in the moonlight.

miyo-nîpin – Good Summer

(singing)

We exchanged breath,
looked into each other's eyes, shared feelings,
talked, laughed of the joys and tragedies of our lives
in the delicate manner of new lovers.

It was a rich summer.
It was a rich summer.

You never know tomorrow's new breath.
It was a rich summer.
It was a rich summer.

Mornings came,
our eyes struggled to open and absorb the light of the Sun,
our souls like newborn birds, ever fragile, ever still.

It was a rich summer.
It was a rich summer.
You never know tomorrow's new breath.
It was a rich summer.
It was a rich summer.

(spoken): It was a rich summer.

(end music)

Summer turned into autumn,
autumn into winter,
the time of the Frost Exploding Trees Moon.

She wasn't well.

At first I thought she was missing her people.
She was pale, and she could not leave our lodge,
for the cold air hurt her lungs.

She developed a cough,
a cough which racked her thin breast,
a cough which brought blood to her lips.

Our healers tried doctoring her.
All through the night their prayers and songs
beseeched the night heavens,
and their spirits travelled far, seeking answers.
Exhausted they returned and said:

It is a sickness we have no cure for
because we have never seen it before.
It comes from across the Big Water.
Maybe she should go back to her people.

(cry)

You must go back, my love, *mon amour.*
niwîkimâkan.
You must go back.

I told her this because I loved her,
and it made me suffer to say it.
But that is how things are with lovers.

After she left, I got sick.
I coughed and I coughed and I coughed.

So I married again, a female from my tribe.
We had many children.
I thought spring would bring me better health.

But my wife began to cough, and so did my children.
All of my relatives became sick.

Spring normally is the time of new life,
when we are happy to be free from the grip of winter.
That year it was filled with the cries of our people
and the bewilderment of not knowing the cause.

It is from exchanging breath with the human, one said.
How could the beauty of our breath cause
something as terrible as this?

I recovered, but my family did not. The snows melted;
I buried all of my loved ones, then all of my tribe.
ALL OF MY TRIBE!

As it was meant to be, I became the Governor.
I accomplished my duties. I fulfilled my destiny as Governor,
not to the living, but to the dead.
The mantle of willow leaves that signified my leadership
I wore not with pride, but with mourning and shame.

The Dead

I did not know the proper rites of the dead
I could not help their joumeys to the Land of the Dead.
I fear that they have not made it to this Land
and are lost somewhere in the In-Between-Land.
Waiting for the day when a true Governor
can help them cross over.

What have I done, will I be forgiven?
What have I done, will I be forgiven?

That spring I sat alone in my village
surrounded by the bones of my tribe,
and the fluttering of the magpies and crows
picking my loved ones' bones.

The dew, they say, is the tears of the Creator.
I am only the Governor of the Dew.
The tears of the Creator for my dead tribe.
Crying for my dead tribe.

What have I done, will I be forgiven?
What have I done, will I be forgiven?

(end music)

ROSE:
mosôm, you have been forgiven many times over.
Through Death, we all have re-found life.

MOTHER:
With that, he cried and cried.
The beaver's tears seemed to be made up of
all the whispering leaves, all the bird songs, all the laughter,
all the brooks and streams in the world.

It was a sound from the beginning of time.
The sound of our Elder Brother as he opened
the little hand of the Muskrat from which the
World was created. This world of suffering and forgiveness.

The beaver's tears opened the doors of Rose Billy's heart,
and she cried the tears of an old woman.
As she cried, she took the ribbons which lay at
the old beaver's feet and wrapped them ceremoniously
around his head, wrists and neck.

For this is how you treat visitors from other worlds,
like Kings and Queens.

NARRATOR:
I think that's how the story goes;
It's been so long since I heard it.
It's from another time, another place,
before I became a man
in this whorehouse of the world.

The old woman who told this story
has passed on,
as did my mother;
this is in memory of them...

êkosi

Guide to the Pronunciation of Cree Dialogue in

Governor of the Dew:

A MEMORIAL TO NOSTALGIA AND LOVE

Jean L. Okimâsis and Arok Wolvengrey

In the following list of the Cree vocabulary found in *Governor of the Dew* an approximate English pronunciation is given for each word, phrase, or sentence, along with a translation. The pronunciation is broken into syllables with primary stress indicated in FULL CAPS, while secondary stress is given in SMALL CAPS. An example of this is as follows:

maskisin . . . . *"shoe, moccasin"*
[MUSS kis SIN]

The Cree word *maskisin,* "shoe, moccasin," thus follows the same stress pattern as the English word "medicine," with primary stress on the first syllable, and a small amount of secondary stress on the final syllable.

Act I

p. 3 **nimâmâ** . . . . *"My mom"*
[M maa MAA]
nikâwiy . . . . *"My mother"*
[NICK COW WEE]

p.4: *Grandmother's Song (repeat twice)*

niya ôma nôcikwêsiw . . . . *"I am the old woman"*
[nee YOH muh noh TSI kway SOO]
Rose Billy kâ-isiyihkâsot . . . . *"The one called Rose Billy"*
[...kaa iss si YEEH kaa SOOT]
ôta niwîkin . . . . *"I live here"*
[oh tuh NI wee KIN]
ê-pêyakowân . . . . *"I am alone"*
[ay pay YUCK koe WAAN]
ê-kaskêyihtamân . . . . *"I am lonesome."*
[ay cuss kay YIH tuh MAAN]
êkwa mîna ê-kitimâkisiyân . . . . *"Also, I am pitiful."*
[ay KWUH mee nuh ay KIT ti maa KISS see YAAN]
êkwa mîna ê-kitimâkisiyân . . . . *"Also, I am pitiful."*
[ay KWUH mee nuh ay KIT ti maa KISS see YAAN]
mah! . . . . *"Listen!"*
[muh]
awîna êtikwê? . . . . *"I wonder who it is?"*
[uh wee NAY tick KWAY]
p. 5: **wahwâ,...** . . . . *"Oh my,..."*
[wuh WAA...]
...'toni nimâmaskâcihon . . . . *"...I was so surprised!"*
[...too NI ni MAA muss KAA tsi HOON]
ê-mamâhtâwahk . . . . *"It was amazing!"*
[ay muh MAAH taa WUHK]
hâm mosôm, tawâw . . . . *"Welcome, grandfather!*
[haam, MOE soom, tuh WOW] *("Grandfather there is room, come in.")*
nôsisê . . . . *"Grandchild"*
[NO say]
mosôm . . . . *"Grandfather"*
[MOE soom]
tâpwê, nôsisê, kitâpwân *"That's true, Grandchild, you speak truthfully."*
[taa PWAY, NO say, KIT taa PWAAN]
kimiyo-pîkiskwân . . . . *"you speak well"*
[ki ME yo PEE kis KWAAN]
hâm, âcimo . . . . *"Tell a story!"*
[haam, AA tsi MOH]

p. 5: **aya, nôsisim** . . . . *"well, Grandchild"*
[eye YUH, NO sim]
cî . . . . *Indicates a question.*
[tsee]

p. 6: **mosôm** . . . . *"Grandfather"*
[MOE soom]
hâm, nôsisim . . . . *"Yes, Grandchild"*
[haam, NO sim]
nitaskiy ôma . . . . *"This is my land"*
[n'tus KEY oh muh]
mâka . . . . *"But,"*
[maa KUH]

p. 7: **wahwâ,...** . . . . *"Oh my,..."*
[wuh WAA...]
...'toni ê-miyohtâkosicik! . . . . *"...they sounded so good!"*
[...too NI ay me YOH taa CO sih TSICK]

p. 9: **namôya konita...** . . . . *"It is not for nothing...*
[nu MOO yuh CONE tuh...]
...mâna kêhtê-ayak k-êtwêcik . . . . *"...that the Elders say,*
[...maa NUH kay TAY yuhk KAY tway TSIK]
ê-âyimahk ôma pimâtisiwin! . . . . *"'life is difficult.'"*
[ay EYE yi muhk oh MUH pi MAA tso WIN]
ê-papâ-môskotêhêyahk . . . . *"We go around with crying hearts."*
[ay puh PAA moos ko TAY hay YUHK]
pôni-mâtoyahk . . . . *"we stop crying,"*
[poe ni MAA toe YUHK]
êkosi ê-pôni-pimâtisiyahk . . . . *"then that's it, we die,"*
[AY ko si ay POE ni PIM maa TIS see YUHK]
nikiskêyihtên êwako! . . . . *"I know that much."*
[nik kis KAY yih tayn AY wuck koe]
kikitimâkisinaw nôsisê . . . . *"We are poor, Grandchild."*
[ki KIT tim maa KISS sin now, NO say]
âstam, kinohtê-pê-wîcêwin? . . *"Come, do you want to come with me?"*
[aahs TUM, ki NOH tay pay WEE tsay WIN]
ê-nitawêyihtamân... . . . . *"I want..."*
[ayn tuh way YIH tuh MAAN...]
...ka-pê-wîcêwiyan . . . . *"...for you to come with me."*
[...kuh PAY wee TSAY we YUN]

p. 10: **kistêsinaw,** . . . . *"Our Elder Brother"*
[kiss TAY sin NOW]
ôma ministik . . . . *"this island"*
[oh muh MIN nis STIK]
niwîkimâkan . . . . *"My wife"*
[ni wee KIM maa KUN]
ôtê ôma kâ-wîkiyân . . . . *"This is where I live."*
[oh TAY oh muh kaa WEE key YAAN]
ôta ôma kâ-kî-pê-ohpikiyân . . . . . . *"This is where I grew up."*
[oh TUH oh muh KAA key pay oh PICK key YAAN]
ôta kîsta ka-wîkin . . . . *"You will live here, too."*
[oh TUH kees tuh KUH wee KIN]

Act II

p. 11: **nôsisim** . . . . *"Grandchild"*
[NO sim]
p. 12: **nôsisê** . . . . *"Grandchild"*
[NO say]
ê-pâstâhoyân . . . . *"I have brought vengeance on myself."*
[ay PAAS taa HOE way YAAN]
mosôm . . . . *"Grandfather"*
[MOE soom]
niya . . . . *"me"*
[nee YUH]
nôsisê . . . . *"Grandchild"*
[NO say]
p. 13: **miyo-nîpin** . . . . *"good summer"*
[me YO nee PIN]
p. 15: **niwîkimâkan** . . . . *"My wife!"*
[ni wee KIM maa KUN]
p. 16: **mosôm** . . . . *"Grandfather"*
[MOE soom]
p. 17: **êkosi** . . . . *"that's it"*
[AY ko si]

p. 8: *Translation of French Song: "Regretter – Regret"*

Translation by Patrick Douaud.

Regretter c'est combattre le temps
et tout au fond des entrailles
un chant d'oiseau à midi.
Si tu pouvais goûter mon coeur,
tu reconnaîtrais le goût
de la cruelle nostalgie,
la solitude de la grand-maman,
de la mûre fraîche de l'été,
de l'amant et de l'aimée.
Ton nom remue d'inconsolables désirs
dans ta sombre forêt,
sous un flou soleil d'hiver
chevaux venant s'abreuver à láube
dans l'ombre de la clairière
le lieu où les guerriers prient.
La solitude de grand-maman,
de la mûre fraîche de l'été,
de l'amant et de l'aimée.
Si tu pouvais goûter mon coeur
tu reconnaîtrais le goût
de la cruelle nostalgie.

To regret is to combat time
from the depths of my being
and the bird's song at noon.
If you could taste my heart,
you'd recognize the taste
of cruel nostalgia,
the loneliness of a grandmother,
the taste of the summer's fresh blackberry,
the distance between the lover and the loved one.
Your name stirs inconsolable desires
in your dark forest,
under a soft winter sun
horses drinking at dawn
in the shade of the clearing
where the warriors prayed.
The solitude of a grandmother,
of the summer's fresh blackberry,
of the lover and the loved.
If you could taste my heart
you'd recognize the taste
of cruel nostalgia.

Acknowledgements

Special thanks goes to Tanya Kappo for her administrative support and friendship, and to Ruth Smillie for her friendship and insight, and to Patricia Favel, Anthony Rozankovic, Peter Smith, Paula Danquert, and Christiane Raby.

ALL MY RELATIVES

Floyd Favel

This play is dedicated to the residents of the Poundmaker Reserve.

characters

ANNA – *a young woman*

GEORGE – *her brother*

ERNESTINE – *the mother*

GRANNY – *the grandmother*

GENEVIEVE – *a Métis woman*

BONIFACE – *Grandmother's younger brother*

All My Relatives was produced by Catalyst Theatre in Edmonton in February 1990, directed by Alan Macinnis and performed by Tantoo Cardinal, Vera Martin, Rhonda Cardinal, Pam Matthews, Floyd Favel and Ron Cook. Special thanks to Ruth Smillie and Alan Macinnis.

Act I – Scene I

Setting: A house on the reserve. Most reserve houses of the time have a front door that opens onto a large room that is both living room and kitchen with no front hall or closet. When the weather's good, the door is usually open to a small porch that these houses have.

GEORGE is sitting in a chair by the door, and looking at the wall. The three women are sitting close together.

ERNESTINE: What happens to us when we start to forget? It's so sad.

GRANNY: Hard times for the one who forgets.

(ANNA and GRANNY nod in agreement.)

GEORGE: *ôta,* along the river valley you used to graze, fight, now you are gone. Where are you? *âskaw mâna,* sometimes when I close my eyes I can almost see you, like a shadow. Snorting, pawing at the ground, making the earth shake like thunder. *êkwa* when I open my eyes I...I can't see you, I forget you. *niwanikiskisin* where are you? *tânitê ê-ayâyan? tânitê ôma ê-ayâyan?*

(The three women who are off to the side speak among themselves, looking at GEORGE.)

ERNESTINE: *(To table.)* All he does is sit and think, he doesn't laugh or play anymore.

ANNA: The little boy left one day and he misses him and I miss him too.

ERNESTINE: Like a wind came one day and took his soul.

(GRANNY hears the sound of horse collar bells. She stops and listens.)

GRANNY: *yaw, awiyak pê-itohtêw,* someone is coming.

(ERNESTINE and ANNA get up to look. GEORGE turns to look. ERNESTINE is trying to make out the figure which is made indistinguishable by the heat waves.)

ERNESTINE: Boniface *cî ana?*

ANNA: Yeah...I think that's him.

GRANNY: *tâpwê?* Sounded like a team of horses.

ERNESTINE: *âsay mîna êtikwê,* he's trying to go home.

(They all sit, ERNESTINE a little stiffly as she rubs her wrists as she talks.)

ERNESTINE: One morning I found him walking down the road, lost. I asked him where he was going, and he said, "I'm trying to go home," to his house which is those rotten old logs down by the creek.

GRANNY: You know, that's where the old people used to live...when they first moved to this reserve...

(GEORGE shows some attention and is listening.)

ERNESTINE: Oh, *tâpwê cî?*

GRANNY: All in one big camp. I remember coming there to visit when we were young, all those old people from another time. I can still see them...their hats, bright kerchiefs, beaded moccasins...

(GEORGE looks around at his surroundings.)

ANNA: They used to live here?

GRANNY: Yeah, if you go walking around there in the bushes, you'll find old things, pots and pans, guns, and if you sit quietly enough, maybe you can hear some whisperings.

ANNA: Whisperings? Of who?

GRANNY: *cîpayak.*

ANNA: The ghosts?

GRANNY: *tâpwê,* sometimes the one who dies stays around. Because they were young when they left...or they left someone they loved...they're restless. Or maybe it's some old person back to have a look around. Sometimes you can hear the ground shake.

ANNA: Shake, from what?

GRANNY: The buffalo, and when it's cold you can see their breath.

(The sound of bells is close now. GEORGE *looks out the window. It's* BONIFACE *and he is looking this way and that. Carrying a harness. He sees* GEORGE *and calls to him.)*

BONIFACE: *nôsisim, âstam.*

*(*GEORGE *gets up slowly and stands to face* BONIFACE *at the door.)*

BONIFACE: *nôsisim, kikî-wâpamâwak cî* my two horses? Two big white mares and *pêyak* black socks *ê-kikiskawât?* All morning *ôma* I'm looking for them, last night *aspin* they took off on me, *âta* I had them buggers hobbled.

GEORGE: *mwâc.* I didn't see nothing.

BONIFACE: Jee Chri. *nititêyihtên* those buggers they came down this-a-way. *mâka* I don't see no damn tracks. *hâw, kiyâm nôsisim, môy kakêtihk nisîpâpêkinên* thank you.

(He turns and continues his search on the cracked dry earth, looking for tracks. GEORGE *goes back to his place by the door and sits heavily.)*

GEORGE: I didn't know he had any horses.

ERNESTINE: He does, he did, about forty years ago.

ANNA: Forty years ago?

ERNESTINE: And he's still looking for them, after all these years.

ANNA: Does he know what year it is?

GRANNY: What do they call *mâna,* when the old people start to forget?

ERNESTINE: Senile, *pakahkam...*

ANNA: Alzheimer's...

ERNESTINE: Or loneliness...there are no borders between yesterday and tomorrow.

GRANNY: *nc!, nîsta* maybe I'm senile.

ANNA: *tânêhki?*

GRANNY: *osâm* all the time I remember things when I was a little girl. *tâpiskôc,* I'm there again, *âskaw mâna* I start to sing this song.

(She sings a little song to herself.)

GRANNY: I don't remember it from anywhere, maybe my grandmother sang it to me when I was young. I can remember the old people visiting and telling things, travelling around by horses. I remember how we were and I begin to miss that.

(GRANNY turns to GEORGE and looks at him. He is off in the room by himself.)

GRANNY: All of them have gone and left us alone to face what will come...they used to say *kî-itwêwak mâna* the priest, that Jesus, he will come back. Why don't you come right now? *tânêhki,* while we still have something.

(She covers her face with her hands.)

GEORGE: Maybe one day it will be better.

(GRANNY looks up at GEORGE.)

GEORGE: *tâpiskôc mâna,* I want to drink where trees drink... *osâm mâna nama kîkway* and there is nothing when I do.

(GRANNY gives GEORGE a drink of water.)

GRANNY: What's wrong?

GEORGE: I used to laugh *môya êkwa*...I can't even think straight.

GRANNY: *tâh-tâpwê,* the old ones hated it when they were moved on to the reserve. They didn't know what was going to happen. Their world ended, all the young men didn't know what to do...*êkwa* when they had the Sun Dance...they had the buffalo skull...it reminded them that there was no more buffalo, and there had been so many. Everywhere they looked they saw empty skies, empty earth, and they said it was like God had left us...alone. There was bones all over, and the government was taking those bones to crush...long trains...of white bones...of death. *(Her voice rises in grief as she speaks for the buffalo.)* And there was no more buffalo...*ê-kitimâkisiyahk...*

ANNA: *nôhkom,* ssh...

GRANNY: *nôsisimak,* don't forget and think that everything is okay. *(She hums the little song she sang earlier and sways back and forth.)* Maybe you think I'm just a silly old woman like my grandmother. She lived that story. I only heard it. Soon you'll leave it beside the road...it will be worse than it is now. Now, the stories are just stories, soon they'll be just foreigner's words. *(No one answers her.) tâpwê,* and it's scary, makes me want to give up. *mâka* what's more scary is not to do anything about it.

GEORGE: So what do you want me to do? Jump on a horse and go on a raid?

GRANNY: You give up?

GEORGE: What else? What am I fighting for? Who am I fighting?

GRANNY: You remember our grandparents, *kimosômipaninawak.* When their world ended what did they pray for? Dance for?

GEORGE: I don't know...I wasn't there.

(GRANNY pauses and thinks.)

GRANNY: When there was nothing, no buffalo, some people down south danced and danced to bring back the buffalo. And they did, they got strength when they fell to the ground after days of dancing. This was the Ghost Dance. They never gave up.

(GEORGE doesn't respond to this. ERNESTINE pours the tea. GEORGE kicks tires.)

GRANNY: *nôhkom mâna,* when she was an old woman, we took care of her. She was very old and from the old days. Sometimes she would get up in the middle of the night and pack all of her things in little bundles. Moving and yelling as if there was dogs and horses around...waking all of us up. She would put all of her things in the middle of the floor and sit on them, and move as if she was travelling. *(She imitates.) mâmaskâc, tânitê êtikwê ê-itâpâsot?* Wonder where she was going. *(She looks to all, closely.) tânitê êtikwê ê-itâpâsot?*

ANNA: *piyis,* it will be night time.

GRANNY: *tâpwê mâka. (She gets up and reties her kerchief. She goes and waves. Everyone waves and ANNA stands watching.) kâwi ôta* this evening I'll come.

(She disappears into the bushes and ANNA *watches her disappear. The sound of her creaking tin pails drifts up through the harsh summer light.*

GEORGE *goes outside. He sees the cracks in the earth because there hasn't been any rain for weeks. He bends to see them closer and traces their patterns with his finger. He looks at his surroundings, as if for the first time.)*

Scene II

(Music fades out. GEORGE *is sitting, sewing coloured ribbons onto a white shirt.* GRANNY *enters after a day of berry-picking and she is surprised to see* GEORGE *wearing two snap-on braids wrapped in fur.)*

GRANNY; *wahwâ,* what long hair you have.

GEORGE: Yeah, I want to be traditional so I can survive.

*(*GRANNY *sits on a chair across from him. She stifles a giggle with her hand.)*

GEORGE: What?

GRANNY: Nothing, nothing...where's your mother?

GEORGE: They went to borrow some sugar.

GRANNY: *kîkwây mâka ê-kaskikwâtaman?*

GEORGE: I'm making a ribbon shirt for dancing.

GRANNY: *miywâsin.*

(She holds her smoking pipe and looks closely at GEORGE *who is busy on his shirt.)*

GRANNY: *piyâhtik,* watch out, *kikiskêyihtên cî tânêhki ohci?*

GEORGE: No. *(He shakes his head, he feels trapped and looks around.)*

(GEORGE shakes his head and GRANNY leans real close, narrows her eyes and whispers menacingly. He backs up against the wall.)

GRANNY: *wîhtikow. (She sits back and listens carefully to the noises outside.)* Yup, you're walking around outside and all of a sudden, you come to a quiet place that makes your hair stand up, like an angry dog's. There is a cold wind that grabs your heart and won't let go. *(She leans over and taps GEORGE's chest with her pipe.)* That's when you know that *wîhtikow* is around. So you better run or pray, or both. Because not an education or a preacher is going to help you there. Just you, that *wîhtikow* is going to eat you up inside, and you yourself will become a *wîhtikow. (She narrows her eyes and looks at him from an angle.) ôta ka-pê-icâscamohcêsin.* You'll come here and you'll look at your relatives in a strange way, and you'll think strange thoughts about them. You'll have to tie yourself up, because it's like you're not yourself anymore, like someone has moved into you and is using your mind, your body...*(She looks at him coldly.)*...someone with an altogether different appetite. One day one of your relatives has his back turned to you, maybe they're making bannock or something, and you sneak up...*(She edges closer to him.)*...and they'll smell so good, like a young deer, or... or...*sîkosâkanak*...mmm...and you'll...you'll... JUMP... *(She leaps to him and grabs him by the shoulders.)*...watch out for that *wîhtikow,* ready to take your mind, your heart. He could be someone offering you money and status, dressed in a nice three-piece suit, or someone you see in the mirror, even your grandmother, *ca.*

(She laughs and slumps in her chair tiredly. ERNESTINE and ANNA come walking in. They have been visiting and they carry a jar of sugar which ANNA places on the table. They sit.)

ANNA: Where's her husband?

ERNESTINE: He's off working somewhere.

ANNA: Doesn't he send her money?

ERNESTINE: He probably does.

ANNA: How come there was no food in the house, then? I hated to take that sugar from them.

ERNESTINE: Me too.

(ANNA looks at GEORGE.)

GEORGE: What's wrong?

ANNA: Nothing, you just look a little sick.

GEORGE: Granny was telling me a story.

ANNA: Must have been some story...what was it?

GEORGE: About *wîhtikow.*

ANNA: *wîhtikow?* I love those stories.

(GRANNY has been sleeping lightly. She raises her head and looks at GEORGE. Just then there is the sound of a truck with no muffler pulling up. It stalls and shudders to a halt. A door opens and slams shut and a voice yells out.)

BONIFACE: *'skanak, kîminîcâkan.* I'd leave you if I didn't have any other but you. *(He kicks the door of his truck.)* You're lucky, you know that? You're lucky *kiyâpic* I still take you around. Next time, my welfare check *takopayiki,* I'll throw you away into the bush. You never treat me good anyway, maybe in the beginning, but now? Oy, yoy, yoy, always acting like you gotta headache. *konita.* You just spend my cheque. *(Everyone has sat down. BONIFACE goes to the window and his face is pressed flat against the window and he is tapping on it.)* Hallo *niwâhkômâkanitik.* Open *ôma* this goddamn door or I'll blow the house down.

ERNESTINE: *nc!, î, ana. (She goes to the door and he enters, shaking his head and speaking quite loud.)*

Boniface: *môy kakêtihk,* I had a hell of a time to get here. *mêskanâhk ana,* my truck act up on me. *(He runs back to the door and shouts out to his truck.)* And don't you take off without me. *(He comes back.)* I treat her nice, *mâka* she's always stopping on me, *tânêhki?* What have I done to deserve this? We get going real good, and I'm happy, *êkot ôhci* headache *k-âyât.* So, she stall on me, right there. But we get here anyways, eh?

Ernestine: What are you complaining about then, *ay-api.*

(Boniface puts his ear close to her mouth.)

Boniface: Ah?

Ernestine: Sit down.

Boniface: Oh, okay. *(He sees Anna and moves towards her, grinning and rubbing his hands together.) wahwâ,* she's getting bigger. Soon, you'll be ready to marry me, *kayâs,* I asked your mother for you, you didn't know that ah? Well, it's true. *âstam,* I want to check how fat you are. *(He tries to grab her and they chase each other about the room. Finally she locks herself in her room and Boniface knocks softly on the door, then kneels down and, taking some candy out of his pocket, he stuffs it under the door.) nah, nîcimos, ka-sîwahcikân. (He stands with difficulty and goes to the table tiredly. He notices Granny, who has been sitting with her eyes resting. He doffs his cap to her and bows politiely.)* Good evening. *(He goes to George and looks at his braids. He signals to Granny.)* When did he get the braids?

George: I decided to be traditional, okay?

Boniface: Good idea.

(He pulls them off to the shock of Ernestine and Granny.)

Boniface: Oh, sorry.

(Granny awakes and makes ready to go. She goes to Ernestine and

GEORGE and shakes their hands and at ANNA's door, she speaks through the door.)

GRANNY: *êkosi,* I'll see you later.

ANNA: Okay *nôhkom.*

(ANNA opens the door slightly, then she sees BONIFACE whose face brightens up. She slams the door shut again. They leave in the truck.)

Scene III

ANNA: Hey George, what ever happened to Danny?

GEORGE: Ah, they moved to the city.

ANNA: And Thomas?

GEORGE: They moved to the city too, just last week.

ANNA: Soon there'll be no one here.

GEORGE: Just old men and women, and dogs, everybody is attracted by the bright lights...the movies...

ANNA: Yeah...and dancing, magazines and good places to hang out, meet all your old friends and relatives looking like models out of a Paris fashion magazine, rapping to the latest hits.

GEORGE: Yeah, right...

ANNA: What do you think about moving to the city?

GEORGE: The city?

(They look in the direction of the city.)

GEORGE: No, we can't, we can't go there.

ANNA: And why not?

GEORGE: It's not traditional to live in the city. Indians aren't supposed to live in the cities.

ANNA: What does living on the reserves, listening to the flies buzzing on the front porch, hearing the dogs bark, have to do with being Indian? If it was only up to me I'd be out of here faster than you could say, *ayapâcinâsihk nicihcîkinêspikêkanênison...*

GEORGE: Haven't you heard, already the cities are being watched. With all those poisons they let in the air, their abuse of power, of electricity, they will be destroyed. It's happened before, it'll happen again. Remember Sodom and Gomorrah.

ANNA: So you're going to hide out here until the end? You might be waiting all of your life. Me, I'm not waiting. Waiting for what? I'm going to go to university in the city and Mom can be near the doctors and be in a good heated house.

ERNESTINE: The cold in the winter blows right through the walls. Now I can't stand it anymore, my bones, you know, get cold and ache even though it feels like fire inside.

GEORGE: You guys have decided on this already.

ANNA: Of course, it's not yesterday that Mom got sick and it's not today that I've thought like this. I've thought like this ever since you started doing nothing...as if you were sick.

GEORGE: I am doing something. I'm making a shirt.

ANNA: So you're going to be a real Indian, uh?

GEORGE: Leave me here.

ANNA: We can't leave you, you'll starve to death.

GEORGE: Someone needs to be here to look after Granny.

ANNA: She doesn't want anybody to look after her yet. If you stayed she'd be looking after you.

(GEORGE looks at ANNA threatening.)

ERNESTINE: You can't cook, what are you going to eat? Fried eggs and fried eggs every day? Who's going to wash your stinking socks?

ANNA: I know, Mom, we'll mail him bannock every week. Come on, Georgie, it'll be fun, you'll meet lots of new friends, girls your age that you can take to movies on those Tuesday night specials, go dancing...besides, it's better for Mom, too...right?

ERNESTINE: *tâpwê...*

(She takes a coat and puts it on GEORGE. She whistles.)

ANNA: Oo wee, hot...you'll drive all the city girls crazy. They'll think, where has he been hiding out all my life? Little did they know, on Poor Blankets reservation. See, look, you look good, urbane...

(He displays himself in the jacket.)

ANNA: Besides, you have to become somebody, you can go to school and do something.

GEORGE: I'll think about it.

Scene IV

(GRANNY is walking around outside her house, kicking dirt and stones with her feet, nudging things that interest her with the toe of her moccasins, or with the thin poplar branch she is carrying, swishing absent-mindedly. She hears the approach of a car and she jogs lightly to the out-house where she stands hidden from view, waiting for the car to pass. The car slows and stops and she sees GEORGE step out. He stands and watches the house briefly. GRANNY steps into view shyly. He is dressed very neat, in a dark coat, and his step seems lighter.)

GEORGE: *nôhkom, tânisi.*

(They shake hands. She extends hers shyly. He extends his arms and moves in a circle, showing off his new outfit.)

GEORGE: What do you think? Sharp, eh?

GRANNY: Yeah, looks good, *tânêhki?*

GEORGE: We're moving to the city. I'm going to be something, a welder...you hear that, a welder.

(Her enthusiasm fails to match his. He looks disappointed.)

GRANNY: Ha, is that right? So everything is solved, eh?

GEORGE: Not only for me, but for Mom, too. She'll be close to the doctors, there's millions of bingos around and she can choose whichever one she wants, like a rich lady. Anna's going to go to university. It'll be better there and we'll be out of this prison.

GRANNY: *tânitê...*

GEORGE: Yah...

(There is a long uncomfortable pause. GRANNY is looking into the bushes.)

GEORGE: It'll be better for us.

GRANNY: You think so. You think so. I think you're like a sheep going to the market. This little sheep went to market, another one...*(She turns and stops.)*...you'll lose yourself in that city...*(She points.)*...those cities aren't ours, you don't belong in there...

GEORGE: Should I live in the bush all of my life?

GRANNY: That city has nice shiny red lips, showing off many good things. You'll go there like sleepwalker...eyes closed...you don't know what you give up. *ôma...(Her hands sweep around.)...ôma...(She points to herself.)...*

GEORGE: Not much.

(She looks at him incredulously.)

GRANNY: *namôya cî kîkway ê-kiskêyihtaman?* What took years and years to build, gone, just like that...*(She snaps her fingers.)*...with that goes your will...your memory. *(She is walking as she speaks.)* God damnit. It's enough those *wîhtikowak* give us a hard time, now we help them do their work. Traitor. *(She stops and picks up something on the ground. It is a beer bottle cap and she holds this triumphantly in GEORGE's face.)* See, even this agrees with me. *(She tosses it disgustedly into the bushes and goes inside her house. He stands, then follows her...knocks on the door.)*

(GRANNY takes some photos which are wrapped in a cloth and she opens these, slowly. She calms down and takes out a photo. She lifts it to GEORGE and he sits across from her.)

GRANNY: *pitawê*...this is your grandfather, Solamoo, *kâ-kî-itiht*, around...1952. *(She sorts through the photos and finds another one.) êkwa awa nôhkom*. She was very old, she had only one eye. *(She closes one of her eyes.)*

GEORGE: How old was she?

GRANNY: Over 100 years old. She used to make medicines and she would tell me what kind to go get in the bush. I would go find them. But I never found out how she made them ready...I never asked, I guess...*(She is listening outside very intently, then shakes her head. She gets up and goes to the window and closes the drapes. She lights a kerosene lamp and shuts off the lights. She places the lamp and sits.)* I heard something in the wind, like whispering...*nîsta* I lost my mom and dad during the sickness in 1918, and I go to live with my oldest sister who was already married. Later, she put me in a boarding school...*(GRANNY is looking far into the wall as she speaks, remembers those times. Her body is frozen in a position. She breaks from her memory and takes another photo and holds it out to GEORGE.) kiwâpamâw cî awa?* That's me when I was in boarding school at Delmas. I stay in there until I'm old enough to marry and I marry your grandpa. We had a big dance that night and boy could I ever jig. They say you couldn't even see my feet. That's how good I was. We worked for farmers in the area, picking roots and stones, clearing brush...One time we went all the way down to Great Falls, Montana, to pick sugar beets...I made friends with some Blackfoot women, but the men, they never got along.... That was a long time ago, those were good times...*(She pauses and looks at GEORGE and pats him on the hand.)*...a road that was necessary, otherwise I wouldn't be the person I am now. I look back and I see this road, a long, dusty, winding one through hills...*êkwa* I see yours...just starting, and who knows what is there for you? You have to go.... *(She gestures ahead and he can almost see the roads that GRANNY has drawn for him.)* You go happy and whistling with your little pack on your back, like a fool, to hard times...before you reach this certain path which not many have found, only the lucky ones...*(She is off on this road.)*

GEORGE: I have to go, or I might as well die.

GRANNY: Each day, look in the mirror and say, "Loneliness, hardship, love, happiness, give them all to me so I can live..."

GEORGE: All of them? *tânêhki?*

GRANNY: Why?...That's good you're moving, a reserve is no good for a Cree, we weren't meant to stay on the reserve, we were always moving, travelling - to live, even though it was hard.

GEORGE: So, it's okay we go?

GRANNY: Yeah, go and find out, maybe you can do something good in the city for somebody. *(She gestures ahead.)* Because you know, the end is coming soon...I can see it. We need to be ready, ready to be standing there in that new life...everything will be new, like a newborn bird...

(GEORGE listens eagerly to this, about the New World.)

GEORGE: The end is coming soon?

GRANNY: Yes, the storms, our people losing their language, all of those are signs...

GEORGE: How will the new world look?

GRANNY: It's hard to say, maybe like the new day or...like springtime when the buds are just starting to open, and you need to be ready.

GEORGE: I will be. *(He stands happily.)* I have to go now, get my things ready.

GRANNY: *cêskwa, cêskwa.*

GEORGE: We're moving tomorrow.

GRANNY: Oh...*sâsay cî, wahwâhay*, don't forget your people, in the end we are all poor, that rich one driving the new car, and that whore on the corner, don't throw any of them away.

(They smile to each other, knowingly. He turns, whistling and dancing down the road. He waves to GRANNY and she waves back. He disappears and her hand drops.

GEORGE exits. GRANNY waves goodbye, enters her house and strikes the lantern and cookie tin.)

Scene V

(ERNESTINE, GEORGE and ANNA are finishing packing up their belongings in big bundles which they will carry. They stop and look at their surroundings, their reserve. GRANNY arrives to say goodbye. She hugs each one and stands, watching. They all start as one, carrying their things. ERNESTINE stops and takes one more look at their home. ANNA comes to her side.)

ANNA: Mom, we'll be coming back.

ERNESTINE: Yeah, but it'll be different...it'll never be the same again...once we go.

(They both stand and watch their house, the trees, the grass where they spent many happy and sad times. GRANNY is a dark figure in the distance.)

ANNA: *êkwa.*

(They turn and they all start off again, ANNA helping ERNESTINE walk down the road. They disappear toward the city.

They arrive at the city, their new home, and they look at all the buildings, the cars, hear the noise.

GENEVIEVE comes walking out of the bar and throws a taunt at someone.)

GENEVIEVE: I'd like to see you come and say that right here...yeah, you better run and don't show your face around here again...

(The family quickly sets up their new home, unpacks, and GEORGE gets ready for his appointment. His mother and sister help him into his jacket and new shoes, and they are proud of him. ANNA hands him his official papers and he is ready to go.)

Scene VI

(GEORGE is sitting in front of an official [BONIFACE] who has his back turned to us.)

GEORGE: Yes, sir? Skipping classes...I haven't been skipping classes...that can be explained...I was sick those days, and I was late for that test because they changed the bus route on me that day. I waited two hours. The other days I had to take my mom to the doctor's...but it's going pretty good this past month, don't you think?...I can get better marks, give me another chance...one last chance.... *(He is stunned for awhile and it takes awhile to find words.)* You're cutting me off my funding 'til next year? What am I going to do for a year?...get a job? Who's going to hire me, I don't have any experience...get welfare? I don't qualify for welfare...Please sir, give me one more chance and I promise I'll do better....*(Official leaves.)* You bastard...

Scene VII

(GEORGE comes out of the Indian Affairs Office and turns to give the building the finger with both hands.)

GEORGE: Let me see you walk in my shoes for awhile! *(He throws his portfolio of papers into the garbage. He looks at the traffic and the dusty streets and his fate dawns on him.)* Oh God...*kîkwây ê-tôtamân. (He puts his head in his hands. BONIFACE comes walking down the street and looks in the garbage bin for empties. He finds a few and deposits them in his bag. He finds GEORGE's papers and takes them too. GEORGE sees him and shakes his head.)*

BONIFACE: Well, well...so...what happened?

GEORGE: They cut off my funding.

BONIFACE: Ah, the Queen is stingy, eh? You know, all my life I hear of the Queen but I never see her...is she in there today?

GEORGE: She lives way across the ocean in a big palace...the ones at the office only work for her...

BONIFACE: Oh...you know, I made twelve dollars this morning, not bad for an old man eh? Hey, since you're not doing something today, why don't you come and help me?

GEORGE: No thanks.

BONIFACE: Well, okay...*nôsisim,* the day is still young and me, not so, and the bottles don't wait, you know...

GEORGE: Okay, see you around.

(BONIFACE turns to leave, remembers the file in his bag, he turns and gives GEORGE back his papers and leaves.)

Scene VIII

(ERNESTINE, GEORGE and ANNA are in the living room. ANNA is helping ERNESTINE get ready to go to bingo. There is a long silence.)

ANNA: Hey Mom, you know what? You remember *pihêw* from the reserve?

ERNESTINE: *mônicâskwêw* daughter *cî?*

ANNA: Yeah, well she's taking a summer class now, and we were having coffee the other day and talking about that tornado that went through the reserve last week. Okay, let's go...*(ANNA helps ERNESTINE into her wheelchair.)*

ERNESTINE: Good thing it missed *kôkom's* house.

ANNA: You know how *pihêw* is sort of a gossip.

Ernestine: Yeah, like her mother...*(Laughs.)...awas,* I shouldn't speak like that.

Anna: She said that none of the good citizens of Poor Blankets were injured. I guess one old man saw the tornado coming, and just before it reached his house, it split in two, passed his house, and hit Johnny Gogo's house where they're always partying...and you know Ralph and *iskwêsip?*

Ernestine: Yeah.

Anna: They say the reason their house was destroyed was because they're first cousins, and they got married...

Ernestine: They say the storms are going to clean up this earth, and all that is no good will be swept away.

George: Yeah? But when? How long do we have to wait, waiting for some sign to brighten our eyes with...hope.

Ernestine: Don't talk like that...it'll happen.

George: But I want it to happen.

Ernestine: *awas...*

George: I want it to happen.

Ernestine: *awas...?*

George: How long have we waited already? And all that greets us is silence and the empty skies, haunted with the ghosts of bleaching bones and rotting corpses. No thunder greets us with rain *pikw îtê ê-pâstêk.*

Ernestine: *tâpwê,* there is no rain here, only the pavement. Maybe we made a mistake in moving here?

Anna: You think so? Things will get better, we just have to be patient, the rains will come.

(BONIFACE comes walking down the street by their house yelling in different tones and inflections, first seductive, then bloodcurdlingly, then joyful.)

BONIFACE: Bingo...bingo...bingo.

(GEORGE yells out the window.)

GEORGE: Shut up.

BONIFACE: *nc!,* but I've gotta practice.

GEORGE: Well, go practice somewhere else, we're talking here.

BONIFACE: This is a free country, I can yell what I want.

GEORGE: No you can't yell what you want.

(BONIFACE talks to the others assembled.)

BONIFACE: I think this boy needs a woman. *(He talks to GEORGE.)* Have I got one for you...I seen her standing just up the street here on 20th...pretty brown eyes...long hair...wait here. I'll go get him.

(GEORGE turns from him and BONIFACE walks down the street. We hear him yell in the distance pitifully.)

GEORGE: No. *awas, niyâ,* go to town.

BONIFACE: Aw...chill out. Bingo.

(ERNESTINE is in her wheelchair. GEORGE gets up and starts to push her out the door.)

ERNESTINE: If you need some money, go pawn the TV...anyways, I'll get it out when my cheque comes.

GEORGE: Sure.

ERNESTINE: Anna, did you talk to that old man for our feast on Saturday?

GEORGE: Why do you wanna have a feast?

ERNESTINE: To say thank you for all the good things we have today, Anna's going to university, you're going to be a welder.

ANNA: Yeah...

ERNESTINE: And I'm feeling so much better...see, I can move this hand now.

(He doesn't answer.)

ANNA: I asked this one elder, but he had to go to a conference, so he can't make it.

ERNESTINE: What about asking Boniface?

ANNA: *nc!,* you got to be kidding, he's so dumb.

ERNESTINE: Don't speak like that, at least he's working.

ANNA: Well, maybe he's a genius in disguise.

ERNESTINE: You know he was raised with *kôkom*. He knows a lot about the old ways.

ANNA: Really?

ERNESTINE: *tâpwê,* so go ask him.

ANNA: All right, but don't blame me if things don't go right.

(ERNESTINE and GEORGE leave. ANNA turns to the mirror.)

Scene IX

(GRANNY is on the reserve. Her house is arranged like a camp and she is looking at the skies and talking to herself.)

GRANNY: *ispîhk ê-kî-wawêsîyân* any time we saw a storm coming, and the Thunder started to call...boom boom, like that...from one cloud to the next one...these were the young ones, they said...or them other kind, just one big boom, like the sky is a drum...*nôhkom mâna,* she would get some herbs and burn them. *(Her story disappears into silence and she sits with bowed head. She looks up again at the horizons.) tânitahto kîsikâw ôta kâ-papêhowân? tânitahto askiy ôta kâ-papêhowân? piyis nikihtimêyihtên ka-pêyakowân, nikihtimêyihtên ka-kaskêyihtamân...*

(ANNA is in the living room in front of the mirror practicing different postures and ways of wearing her hair, and practicing her speaking.

ANNA: Hi...hi...hello...hello...well, hello there...hi there, hello there...no kidding...really? *(She covers her mouth and giggles coyly.)*...one never knows...hi...hi to you too...

(GEORGE enters and she stops, embarrassed.)

ANNA: You take Mom to bingo?

GEORGE: Where else? *(He goes to the window.)* How does...a warrior live in this...this...castrated age...without a horse, without a gun?

(ANNA goes over to him.)

GEORGE: How does a real heart survive in this desert? Look, nothing real can grow there, there's no roots. How can roots survive...in concrete?

ANNA: Are you trying to tell me you're not going to school?

GEORGE: Yeah, they cut off my funding. *(He makes a motion across his throat.)*

ANNA: You were RTD'd...why?

GEORGE: *awas êkosi,* it's policy.

ANNA: Did you tell Mom?

GEORGE: Not yet.

ANNA: Can't we do something about it?

GEORGE: When they say no, it means no.

(Pause.)

ANNA: If they knew there was nothing out there for you, maybe they'd change their minds?

(He hits the wall. Pause.)

GEORGE: Shit...what am I going to do? Can't get a job, can't get welfare...don't have an old lady to move in with and support me...just a damn cast off...who's going to want me? I'm an undesirable.

ANNA: I don't know...somebody might find you desirable. *(She laughs at her own joke. GEORGE gives ANNA a threatening look.)* Just joking...let's go pawn the TV, I got a class this afternoon.

GEORGE: I know how those Palestinians feel...refugees in our own country...living in these...camps, reserves...I'm just about ready to go throwing rocks and molotov cocktails...boy, I should of gave them a punch...I should of swore more...

(ANNA has begun to unplug the TV.)

ANNA: And, they'll never fund you again...

GEORGE: That'll be the price, at least I went down fighting...

(She has the TV ready.)

ANNA: Out with a bang...not a whimper...that's a real warrior...

GEORGE: I wish it was more simple...hunting, fishing...fighting hand to hand...*(He comes over to help her.)*

ANNA: *wâ,* as if you were there...

GEORGE: Wish I was...

(They go walking down the street.)

GEORGE: Wishing I was...dying bravely, not like a dog in the street...if there was a Ghost Dance you know what I'd do?

ANNA: What?

(They put the TV down and GEORGE describes with large gestures.)

GEORGE: I'd take my white shirt with colored ribbons...then I'd paint this big, big star in the front, with blue, and there would be planets and stars in an arc like this...then I'd dance, dance out of this awful world.

(He makes a gesture and closes his eyes and dances slowly in a circle.)

GEORGE: Boy, they are butchering cows up there.
kwêyask osihtâ arrow straight
arrow *osihtâ,* make an arrow
and you better be straight
so you can fly...

(He makes a gesture and closes his eyes and dances slowly in a circle. He falls down to the street and ANNA rushes over and sits beside him.)

ANNA: George? What's wrong?

GEORGE: I don't know...it's like I want to cry.

ANNA: You can if you want. *(She holds him and rocks him back and forth. After awhile, she gets up.)* Come on, let's go.

(He gets up slowly and dusts off his clothes and helps her with the TV*. They walk down the street and see an old friend of theirs from the reserve.)*

GEORGE: There's Raymond, the one you had a crush on in grade six.

*(*ANNA *can't believe the changes that have taken place in Raymond, the years of drinking and unemployment.)*

ANNA: No, that's not him.

GEORGE: Yes, it is.

ANNA: No, it isn't.

GEORGE: It is, see, I'll call him.

ANNA: No, don't call him, come on...

(They continue walking and ANNA *gives one backwards glance at him. They see another person they know. A young woman standing on the street.)*

ANNA: Isn't that Genevieve Larocque? Your old *kîcimos?*

GEORGE: Boy, she's changed.

ANNA: For better or for worse?

(He turns to look at her.)

GEORGE: Both.

ANNA: She's sure looking good.

*(*GENEVIEVE *sees them and comes walking over.)*

GENEVIEVE: Is that a walk or a broken hip?

GEORGE: A walk...

(They embrace.)

GENEVIEVE: You got time to buy an old friend a drink? Like the old days, when...you used to ride over when everyone was gone and...we'd...

GEORGE: Yeah...I remember...how could I forget...

GENEVIEVE: ...have some beer...listen to CCR, and you'd tell me all your plans. *(She circles GEORGE and she is quite near to him by now.)* Well, *kayâs...(She sings in GEORGE's ear.) Long as I remember, rain's been coming down...remember that?*

GEORGE: Yeah, I do.

GENEVIEVE: Anna, how're you doing?

ANNA: Fine, what are you up to now?

GENEVIEVE: Oh, I'm working at the Centre. I've been there about a year, how long you guys been in town?

ANNA: Not long. I'm going to university.

GENEVIEVE: Hey, good for you. George...?

GEORGE: Um, uh, we have to be going. Let's get this home.

GENEVIEVE: You know what, your brother here would bring me bouquets of crocuses. I remember that one time we found a tiger lily in the bush?...and we took care of it like it was our child...we went there one morning and someone had picked it, so we both cried.

ANNA: Those were the good old days.

GENEVIEVE: He used to whisper his Cree poems to me, how did that one go? *kiya ôma kâ-sâkihitân, namôy wihkâc nasipwêhtân, niwâpikwaniy, niwâpikwaniy*...remember when Emil took a dive into the creek, and the water was only knee high?

ANNA: Uh yeah, I remember that.

GENEVIEVE: Let's all get together sometime, and remember the old days.

GEORGE: Before we become refugees.

GENEVIEVE: Oh, George, you haven't changed.

GEORGE: Come on, we've got to be going. *(ANNA glares at GEORGE.)*

(GENEVIEVE starts to leave.)

GENEVIEVE: *(Speaking over her shoulder.)* George, meet you at the Albany at nine...and we'll hit a few bars.

Scene X

(GEORGE is in a loud smokey bar full of staggering people. GENEVIEVE enters and yells to BONIFACE.)

GENEVIEVE: Two draft.

GEORGE: Nice place.

GENEVIEVE: This place? This place is a dive.

(A waiter comes [BONIFACE] and GEORGE makes a motion to pay.)

GENEVIEVE: No...this one's on me. *(She pays and the waiter leaves. He and GEORGE exchange glances.)* So you quit school, and what are you up to now?

GEORGE: Now...? I decided to start my own business.

GENEVIEVE: Oh, really...what kind?

GEORGE:...I'm a travel agent and a promoter.

GENEVIEVE: A travel agent and promoter?

GEORGE: Yeah...it's called All My Relatives Agency...

GENEVIEVE: What do you do?

GEORGE: I book tours, you know big tour buses and all that...

GENEVIEVE: Oh, really...

GEORGE: Of course, I'm just getting it off the ground now, basically it's still a concept. *(She looks at him questioningly. GEORGE is a bit uncomfortable.)* Yes, sir, that's how it is. *(He laughs nervously.)* Let's get out of here.

(GENEVIEVE and GEORGE come unsteadily out of the bar, arm in arm.)

GENEVIEVE: Yeah, sure, I got to go home and get some sleep anyways, I work tomorrow...

GEORGE: Well, I'll go with you. I'm leaving town soon.

GENEVIEVE: Leaving, where?

GEORGE: I got to go to a rodeo down south in Maple Creek. I ride bulls, too, you know. *(He flexes his wrist and pulls an imaginary rope.)*

GENEVIEVE: Ride 'em cowboy.

GEORGE: When I win we can move in together, get a VCR and stay home on weekends and see movies.

GENEVIEVE: Move in? Holy, boy, you move fast...

GEORGE: Well, why not?

GENEVIEVE: I thought you were a businessman?

George: I am, and a cowboy too.

Genevieve: Well, when you get back give me a call. *(She turns.)* Taxi.

George: Wait, where you going?

Genevieve: I already told you, I'm going home.

George: I'll go with you. Taxi.

Genevieve: Wow, you're one tough warrior. *(The taxi goes by without stopping.)* I'm a warrior, too, so don't mess with me. My great-grandfather fought at Batoche...and I'm named after my great grandmother...Genevieve Larocque. Taxi. *(She hails a taxi and turns to go.)*

George: Wait, don't go now.

(She shakes off his hold.)

Genevieve: Don't fucking grab me like that. We're not kids anymore. *(She walks to the taxi.)* George, call me under Larocque. Avenue M, South.

(She leaves, leaving George standing on the street watching the taxi.)

Scene XI

(It is the middle of the night and Granny is packing and loading up all of her things. She thinks she is breaking camp and moving to better pastures.)

Granny: *awas wîn-atim...yîkatêhtê...(She calls to some old person walking by.) nôhkom,* where's that pinto? He's the only one that's any good for carrying the tent...*na, pihêw* is riding him? *cah,* but he's old...he'll ride him to death...*(She turns to some children fooling around.) hâm mâka kîsta, wîcihtâso...*

what do you think this is, a damn picnic?...*niyâ,* you go over and get that bitch with the white eye and bring her here, *kiyipa.* We don't have all day...

(She sees her dad riding by. She gets bored with travelling and asks her dad. She asks like a young girl.)

GRANNY: *nôhtâ,* how much longer? I wish we were there...I'm tired, I'm cold...

(She curls up on her things, whispering to herself, listening to the sounds of the night, seeing the moon. The lights fade to black.)

Act Two – Scene I

(It's morning and ANNA enters the house, just returning from the hospital. ERNESTINE is waiting for her.)

ERNESTINE: What did they say?

ANNA: They didn't really know, but they said she's under observation...they found her early this morning laying on all of her stuff in the middle of the room. Do you think she'll die?

ERNESTINE: I don't know, it's not for me to say.

(ERNESTINE shrugs and ANNA gets up to look out the window.)

ANNA: The moon was full last night. Granny said that that's where the dead people go. Last night I was laying down and slowly the light was climbing up, covering me like a silver blue blanket...and I didn't know if I was living or dead, I knew something was going to happen...Maybe it's better up there...Mom, you think so?

(ERNESTINE doesn't say anything and ANNA goes back to looking outside.)

Ernestine: *awas,* don't talk like that...

Anna: I'm not scared of dying. There's nothing to be afraid of...I'm more afraid for us who are living.

(George enters the house looking very hung over. He sits tiredly on the sofa and there is a long silence.)

Ernestine: You're late for school. If you start drinking, you'll get kicked out.

George: I'm already kicked out.

Ernestine: When?

George: A few days ago...

Ernestine: So what are you going to do?

George: I don't know...be a bum.

Ernestine: If you're going to be a bum, you can't stay here. I don't want to live with any bums.

(George returns to his room.)

Anna: George...Granny is in the hospital.

George: *tânêhki?*

Anna: They don't really know. She was trying to go somewhere, and she just collapsed. An ambulance brought her in this morning.

George: Where is she now?

Anna: St. Peter's...

(George leaves the room quickly.)

Anna: Wait.

ERNESTINE: Go with him...go. You can take me later.

ANNA: *(Leaving.)* I'll be back soon. George...

Scene II

(GRANNY is in her hospital bed, having a conversation with someone.)

GRANNY: Here I am an old lady but I haven't done my true turning, my true turning...Never mind me...what about my grandchildren...they have so little, like beggars...

(ANNA and GEORGE have listened to the last part of her words and they enter the room quietly.)

GEORGE: *nôhkom.*

GRANNY: *namôya, namôya, pitamâ.*

ANNA: Granny, it's me Anna...

GRANNY: St. Anne?

ANNA: Anna...

GRANNY: *(She looks to ANNA and laughs.)* I thought St. Peter was calling me...then St. Anne.

GEORGE: And here's St. George, ready to kill a dragon...and with the breath of a dragon too....

GRANNY: *apik.(She motions them to sit.) nôsisim,* get my tobacco out of my jacket there, this calls for a smoke...this visit.

(GEORGE gets the tobacco and GRANNY pulls out her pipe and he gives her the tobacco.)

GRANNY: Thank you, you're a gentleman, I see. You learn in the bar? Boy, I should get sick more often. *(She prepares her pipe contentedly.)* Today I walked over to that window there, to smoke, *kiyâm* if this hospital is non-smoking, *nêhiyaw ê-kî-miyikowisit cistêmâs.* Looking out on the streets where my grandchildren live...and I could see what you were doing, like some angel watching. I wonder what it is like to be an angel? *(She moves her arms like wings and makes a whistling sound.)* The smoke takes our words and thoughts up for all and everything to hear...You can't fool Him, *wiya,* the One and Only, the one and only, *wiya,* he is our king, our Prime Minister. Don't fool your friends, but most of all don't fool yourself. Don't be one of the sheep the Good Shepherd hypnotized so he could eat them up...*âhkamêyimok.* There once was a Shepherd whose sheep were always getting away on him, and he thought about what he should do. So, he hypnotized all of them and told them there is no reason to escape, life is good here. And the sheep were content and stayed. Whenever the shepherd got hungry, he would slaughter one of the sheep and roast him...one day one of the sheep realized they were hypnotized, so he escaped. *(She looks at them. She blows the smoke in their direction deliberately.)* Are you that sheep?

(GEORGE shrugs.)

GRANNY: Everything around us is whispering, it's time...it's time...you hear it in the grasses, in the birds singing, in the people's suffering. We need to wake up and see. The new day is coming, soon.

ANNA: What are the signs?

(GRANNY looks out the window and it appears she has not heard.)

GRANNY: When the time comes that Indians don't speak their languages anymore, that's one sign of the end. *kayâs,* there was a time when everyone spoke the same language, and they thought they were something. *ê-mistakêyimisocik* so they built this big tower, the Tower of Babel to reach

Heaven, and God punished them for their pride.... It's like that now, eh? Everybody is speaking the same language and their pride is going to destroy this world. You agree?

GEORGE: *môy nikiskêyihtên*...I don't know.

GRANNY: A jackass mumbles if he has a mouth full of oats. I don't know...a warrior gives a strong answer, *ahâw*.

(GEORGE leaves the room angrily, slamming the door.)

GRANNY: He doesn't look too happy.

ANNA: Everything's been going wrong for him.

(She laughs.)

GRANNY: Well, I better not die yet...*kiya mâka, tânisi,* how are you?

ANNA: Oh, I'm still in classes.

GRANNY: *ho, kîkwâya?*

ANNA: Psychology and Religious Studies. Lately we've been reading about the Chinese. You know, their ways are like ours, only they call theirs the Tao.

GRANNY: Tao? *kîkwây mâka.*

ANNA: There is no one meaning for it, because if it could be put into words it wouldn't be Tao anymore.

GRANNY: *tâpwê cî?*

(She adjusts herself into a more comfortable sitting position.)

ANNA: It's like a river from Nowhere that flows into Nowhere, and we should be a part of this river, letting it carry us along, gently. Like we're a boat on a river, letting ourselves be guided by this river.

Granny: A river, *sîpiy*.

Anna: So, it means, I think, not forcing anything, put things and places in their proper time and place. Things being as they are...essential...and simple.

(She says this softly and her body moves as if she is rowing a boat. Her arms are raised in a rowing position.)

Granny: Can we row the boat?

(Anna laughs.)

Anna: Of course not, silly goose...then it wouldn't be Tao any-more.

(Granny tries again, this time without oars.)

Granny: *miywâsin* this Tao, you should tell your brother about it.

Anna: Yeah, but I don't want to force anything on him, it's just not...Tao.

Granny: All right. We better finish now. I'll live and if I don't, then I don't, that's Tao, *cî?*

Anna: Right. How did you know?

Granny: Oh...experience.

(Anna starts to leave, and stops and turns at the door.)

Anna: Get well, Granny, we need you.

Granny: Sure you do.

(Anna leaves and Granny gets up and looks out the window at her walking down the street. She waves.)

Scene III

(George is walking heavily down the street, very depressed. Anna catches up to him.)

Anna: Is that a walk or a broken hip?

(George spins around eagerly.)

Anna: George?

(They see their people on the street. George rushes forward, yelling.)

George: *âhkamêyimok*. The end is coming. We don't know the day or the hour.

(Anna grabs him and tries to quiet him.)

Anna: George. *(She turns to a passerby.)* It's okay, he's just...happy, aren't you? *(She laughs nervously and George breaks free.)*

George: Listen to me. Already the axe is laying at the root of the tree. Ready to cut down those that don't bear good fruit.

(They struggle as Anna has her hand over his mouth and his head in a headlock.)

Anna: Ssh, who do you think you are?

George: We don't know the day...or the...

Anna: John the Baptist? *(She throws him to the ground and covers his mouth.)* Ssh, you'll get arrested.

George: It's okay, when I saw all of our people, I was just moved to speak.

Anna: By what? The Holy Spirit?... It's going to get you in trouble.

GEORGE: It always gets us in trouble.

(They lie on the street for awhile, catching their breath. ANNA looks at the people and says to GEORGE.)

ANNA: Look at our people, their smiles, their poorness, aren't they beautiful?

(GEORGE looks up.)

ANNA: The people that we have thrown away...*iskonikanak* in robes of rags, walking the streets, paved over our tears.... See those ladies? They're royal princesses.

GEORGE: The ones in the pink stretch pants?

ANNA: Yeah, imagine they are happy, and there's no city here, just grass for miles around, as far as we can see or hope.

(They look for a while and ANNA helps him up and dusts him off.)

ANNA: Come on, I have to take Mom to Bingo.

(They walk down the street.)

GEORGE: *kôhkominaw* was hard with me.

ANNA: Because she loves you.

GEORGE: That's a strange way to show it.

(A car roars by and a voice yells out.)

VOICE: Hey you squaws, how much?

(The car drives off and GEORGE looks down at himself.)

GEORGE: Fuck you. Come here and say that. Jeez, the nerve.

ANNA: Maybe it's the way you walk.

GEORGE: Is that a compliment or an insult?

ANNA: How do you like being called a squaw?

(He walks and looks at himself.)

GEORGE: I'm proud. Go ahead. Call me a squaw...call me two squaws.

(They encounter ERNESTINE *on the road.)*

ANNA: Mom, how did you get here?

(They are walking by the Bingo Palace and ERNESTINE *is sitting outside the door. They go to her.)*

ERNESTINE: Baptiste came by and dropped me off here. How is *kôkom?*

ANNA: Cranky as usual. But she's stable. They're gonna do some tests.

ERNESTINE: I'll go see her tonight.

GEORGE: *tânisi,* here's a cigarette, offer it to the bingo spirit, and if you win, I get half, *ca*.

ANNA: Did you smudge your bingo dabbers?

*(*ERNESTINE *takes their remarks with good humour.)*

ERNESTINE: Couldn't wait. I feel lucky today, my hand is twitching right here. *(She points to a place on her right hand.)*

ANNA: Means you're going to win.

ERNESTINE: Maybe I will. That's all we have, good luck.

(They arrive at the bingo hall.)

ERNESTINE: *wâ,* look at all these people coming to bingo. This must have been how it was a long time ago, when the buffalo came by a camp, just going and going...looks like welfare day...

GEORGE: Will the buffalo ever come back?

ANNA: If they came back where would they stay?

ERNESTINE: They say the buffalo will always be here, don't worry...maybe not wild, but on a reserve...like us.... They'll always watch over us, they say. *ki-îtwêwak mâna,* when life was good for the Indian people, his four legs were planted firmly in the ground, like trees. Then, when the priests came and started to divide us with their faiths, the buffalo sacrificed one of his legs so we could go on living.... When we moved to the reserves and had no hope, he sacrificed another leg for us, and he had to stand as best he could on only two legs...He was getting weak, and when the grandchildren began to turn their backs on their language and old people, the buffalo lost another leg for us so we could keep on living. He knew that if he failed there would be no hope for us, so he gathered all of his strength and stood his ground. There he stands today, on just one leg, trying to do his best.

Scene IV

(GENEVIEVE and GEORGE are sitting in the park, drinking. GENEVIEVE pours some beer on the ground.)

GENEVIEVE: These are the last two, George. Hey, my uncle used to do this. Hey uncle, here's to you. Hey, come, celebrate, we only live once.

(GEORGE doesn't answer and sits silently. He too pours some on the ground.)

GENEVIEVE: He had a drinking song,...*ê-minihkwêyahk,*

okîsikowak kikanawâpamikonawak...they sure knew how to party. Hey, this is to life.

(They toast each other.)

GEORGE: How can you laugh when we are so poor, *ê-kitimâkisiyahk?*

GENEVIEVE: How can you not?

GEORGE: I'm thinking of the buffalo and how they died as they did, with no respect and left to rot in the grass...or shot just for sport...and if they could speak to us, what would they say? *kîkwây kê-itwêwak?* There is no one to speak for them, but I can hear their voices across those hundred years. *kikitimâkisinânaw,* the tears they didn't cry and the tears of our people who watched them die like that, want to come out...

(GENEVIEVE hugs him.)

GENEVIEVE: George, grief makes us sick if we keep it in, when the grief comes out we are getting stronger.

GEORGE: I know, but it makes me want to die.

GENEVIEVE: You're learning to live.

GEORGE: Why does it have to be so hard?

(They're silent for awhile.)

GENEVIEVE: Are you crying for the buffalo or are you crying for yourself? If you cry too much and too long, it becomes self pity.

GEORGE: Self pity?

GENEVIEVE: Yes, grief should make you want to get up and do something great...come on, enough of this bullshit...

George: I gotta go.

(He grabs his jacket and runs. She stops him and she tries to pull him back.)

Genevieve: Where are you going?

George: I have to go to a feast with my family.

Genevieve: A feast? You can't go to a feast...you're drunk.

George: That doesn't matter, I want to be there.

Genevieve: You're showing disrespect.

George: To who? The spirits see me already like this.

Genevieve: Of course they see us, we gave them a drink didn't we. I mean your family. You're showing disrespect to them.

George: No, my family has to take me as I am, see me in every way.

Genevieve: Wait, I'll come with you.

(They go.)

Scene V

(Anna, Ernestine and Boniface are dressed in their best. There is a blanket spread out in the middle of the floor and they are waiting for someone.)

Boniface: Well...there once was this rich landlord whose son was getting married, so he made this big feast and invited all the important people of the area. On the day of the wedding he waited, but no one showed up. Finally, a messenger came galloping up and he said his master couldn't make it that day, as something important had come up. Then another one came, saying almost the same thing. Then the landlord knew that no one was going to show up. He got angry and he called his servant and told him, "Go out into the streets and invite the poor, the sick, all that you can find, and tell them a feast is here waiting for them." So the servant left...

ERNESTINE: Did he know the feast was today?

ANNA: Yes, he was with me when we asked Boniface.

(BONIFACE nods affirmatively. He is relishing his role as a respected elder. He smooths out the cuffs of his jacket.)

ERNESTINE: We might as well start...don't you go inviting your friends.

(She says this to BONIFACE.)

ANNA: You want me to be a server?

ERNESTINE: *êtikwê.*

ANNA: Even though I'm a woman?

ERNESTINE: Well, there isn't any man around here.

(BONIFACE removes his coat with a flourish and is about to sit, when he stops.)

BONIFACE: You know, I almost didn't make it here today. I met this born again Christian Indian, and he almost converted me, until...

(He waits for a response.)

ANNA: Until what?

BONIFACE: Well, he just kept speaking and smiling, so I waved my hand in front of his face, like this...*(He waves his hand in front of his face.)*...and I yelled *waniskâ,* wake up...but he thought I was calling on the devil when he heard me speak Cree, so he took off on me, faster than a two dollar bill...so fast he jumped out of his pants and left them...

(BONIFACE pulls his pants down revealing another pair underneath. ANNA laughs.)

BONIFACE: See...

ERNESTINE: *awas, kiyipa,* Boniface.

(BONIFACE starts to sit down on the floor grandly and elaborately, but stops himself halfway down. He stands up.)

BONIFACE: You know, my old man was a crazy old bugger...

ANNA: How crazy was he?

BONIFACE: He was so crazy that whenever they went to town, his wife made him wear a straight jacket.... Compared to my old dad, I'm like a judge going home from an AA meeting. One time, I was with him at a feast. It was outside and he was blessing the food that day. Well me, you know, I had my head bowed and my eyes closed real tight, praying like a son-of-a-bitch. Then, way over on this side of the west, I hear thunder. I open one eye and seen these dark clouds coming fast. I thought, this old bugger better hurry up, but he kept on and on...and me, I just kept praying like a bat out of hell. Soon it started to rain, but my dad kept on praying. *piyis* I was soaked, everyone was soaked. So, finally, I yelled really loud, Hurry Up Harry...because Harry was his name. He just looked at me and I could see this little smile on his face, and he kept on praying.... And me? By this time I was all prayed out.... Soon we were sitting in this lake and all the food was floating on top...

Ernestine: Hurry up Boniface.

Boniface: By the time he finally finished blessing the food, all the food had floated away...so me and my friends stole a boat, but we didn't get far...

(Ernestine yells, mimicking Boniface.)

Ernestine: Hurry up Boniface.

(Boniface gets ready to begin, when George and Genevieve enter arm in arm.)

George: *tânisi niwâhkômâkanitik,* forgive me.

Genevieve: I tried to get him not to come, I told him it isn't right.

George: I've thought about what you said and what you said this past night, and I know that being drunk isn't the way to be, but here I am because I love all of you. Mom, *anohc niminihkwân, kâya nânitaw itêyihta. namôy kihtwâm nika-minihkwân.*

(He goes to Ernestine and kneels in front of her.)

George: *tâpwê,* mom, *môy kihtwâm.*

Ernestine: *atimociskak,* get the hell out of here...

(She tries to hit George but her wheelchair won't allow her.)

George: *tânêhki.*

Ernestine: Can't we do anything right? Just because we're living here, it doesn't mean that we have to forget the way things are done. We try, we cook all day, get some food together, clean up the house, dress ourselves up and think about the good things today, how lucky we are to be alive...and you show up drunk.

(There is a long silence.)

BONIFACE: Let them stay, we can't refuse anybody, that's not our way.

ERNESTINE: Tell me where it says the drunken?

ANNA: Mom, let them stay, no matter what we can't turn anyone away.... They wouldn't be here if they weren't meant to be...

(They all remain standing in silence.)

ERNESTINE: *hâm mâka.*

BONIFACE: Hokay, let us commence the feast.

(ANNA goes into the kitchen and comes back with a pot of food. BONIFACE eyes the contents hungrily and tries to peek under the lid.)

BONIFACE: *ânakacâ.*

GENEVIEVE: I'm sorry...

(She offers her hand to ERNESTINE and ERNESTINE accepts.)

Scene VI

(GEORGE and ANNA are in a bar.)

ANNA: Here I am.

GEORGE: Finally.

(GEORGE is dressed in denim with a belt with a big, beaded buckle and a choker. Anna is carrying a camera.)

George: How do I look?

(He walks around and takes a stance against the door, his fingers hooked into his belt.)

Anna: All right, so what do you want me to do?

George: Take some pictures of me here and there, these are my promotional pictures.

Anna: In a bar?

George: Not only in a bar, but in other places. See, I invite non-native people to come and see us, for a price. I take them around to contemporary urban Indian families and they see how we live. I give them a light lunch, they see our beauty. Visit All My Relatives, tours offered daily, by a real urban native guide.

Anna: Get your own welfare cheque with your name on it.

George: Yeah, good idea. *êkwa,* let's go.

Anna: You ready?

George: Wait. *(He looks around for someone.)*

Anna: Looking for a dancing partner? What about that one? She looks quite native.

George: No, not urban enough. I need one with...panache.

(Genevieve comes walking in.)

Genevieve: Sorry I'm late.

George: No problem. No, I kinda like to have a beer first.

Genevieve: This song? Can't I have a beer first?

George: Later, first we'll dance.

(They dance and ANNA is off to the side taking pictures. Every time she takes a picture, all the action and lights stop.)

GENEVIEVE: What is going on?

GEORGE: For my new business. You were great. I just need a few promotional pictures.

GENEVIEVE: Okay...

(They continue dancing and ANNA takes some more pictures.)

SCENE VII

(GRANNY is lying in her hospital bed. The radio is playing with some static. The music stops.)

RADIO: Environment Canada has issued a tornado warning for the area as funnel clouds have been sighted northwest of the city, causing extensive damage to farm machinery and buildings. Some livestock were reportedly destroyed...

(The radio crackles to a halt and it goes off the air. GRANNY rises slowly, listening, and goes to the window. What she sees frightens her.

Meanwhile, GEORGE is nervously pacing up and down the street in front of his mother's house. He looks at his watch, then looks at the sky. He speaks to GENEVIEVE.)

GEORGE: Looks like it's going to rain.

GENEVIEVE: What time did you say they were coming?

GEORGE: Right at six.

GENEVIEVE: These are the ones from West Germany?

George: No, that's tomorrow, these ones are from Fort Lauderdale, retired people.

(Ernestine and Anna come out of the house.)

George: Hey, where are you going?

Ernestine: Bingo.

George: Don't go now, can you just sit around for awhile drinking tea and smoking, Anna I thought you were going to make bannock...I have some friends coming in soon.

Ernestine: This is your tour guide stuff.

George: Yes, you don't have to do much, I'll pay you.

Ernestine: I don't want to be like some animal in a zoo, *êkwa* let's go, and don't take them inside my house.

(She and Anna leave. There is a low, ominous roar of thunder and the wind rises.)

George: Oh, my God. There's the bus from Fort Lauderdale.

Genevieve: So what are you going to do?

George: We'll take them to your place.

Genevieve: My place, no way.

George: Only for a few minutes, all you have to do is sit around and act natural.

(The storm gets louder.)

Genevieve: Why don't you take them down 20th, stop in front of the Albany and the Dakota restaurant.

George: But it's raining.

GENEVIEVE: Then give them a tour of the bingo hall, whatever, just say, "These are my people and I take them as they are."

GEORGE: It's not what I promised in the brochure. And I can't break my promise.

(GENEVIEVE signals to GEORGE and they both turn and see the approaching tornado. There are sounds of destruction and they are frozen in place, watching. The wind rises, there is hail and rain…and the power goes out.)

Scene VIII

(B[illegible]IFACE has gone speechless, but he tries to explain what had happene[illegible] [illegible]he place is in a shambles. BONIFACE is frantically trying to commu[illegible] what he saw and how he tied himself to the fridge so he wouldn't b[illegible]d up, and how they were whirled around and around and wound up [illegible]he street.

ANNA is trying to interpre[illegible]tions with words. He nods furiously every time ANNA guesses correctl[illegible]

ANNA: Calm down, calm down, j[illegible]st show us what happened.

(BONIFACE starts his mime.)

ANNA: A big funnel cloud...

(He nods furiously at ANNA. GENEVIEVE pushes ERNESTINE in a wheelchair and GEORGE enters.)

ANNA: That was easy...so you took a rope, no...Granny's pantyhose?

ERNESTINE: *cwâ…*

ANNA: Well, I think that's what he said...and the fridge fell on you, no...you tied yourself to the fridge, yes? Okay...and a big hand...the hand of God?...No?...Whirled you around and around...and...you thought...you would never see daylight again, right?

GENEVIEVE: You went to Hawaii.

ANNA: You floated down...like...like...your mother used to lay you down...and you passed out...

(He nods a negative.)

ANNA: You fainted...someone was licking you...a dog was licking your face...

(BONIFACE turns quiet, ANNA comes closer to him, he has fallen asleep.)

ANNA: He's been like that ever since the tornado.

ERNESTINE: I wonder if he'll ever speak again?

ANNA: I think it's probably just shock.

(They sit quietly.)

ANNA: I'm glad you made it home safe.

ERNESTINE: Me too, didn't think I would for awhile. There was bingo cards and Nevada tickets flying around like a snowstorm. The windows were broken, and I seen the bingo caller get thrown into the concessions...yeah, and there was still some people in all this trying to grab these Nevada tickets.... If we had died, some of us would've died happy...and gone to the Bingo Palace in the sky...

GENEVIEVE: Have you ever seen a tornado before?

ERNESTINE: No, but I remember when I was young, this old woman used to come and visit us from down south. She said that sometimes the wind got so strong they had to tie themselves to trees...and one time she saw this cow flying through the air.

*(*ERNESTINE *makes a big arc across the sky showing the path the cow took.* BONIFACE *wakes and nods that this is what happened to him also.* ANNA *soothes him and calms him, speaking to him like she would to a child.)*

ANNA: Ssh...sh...*âmî...âmî*...remember what Granny said...if you're straight and good, and follow that straight and narrow path, then you don't have to be afraid...understand?

(He nods.)

ANNA: Good...all these big storms are cleansing...then everything will be clean and pure again...we can drink the water from the rivers again...all the animals will come back...we'll see whooping cranes flying north...with their long white wings...and we'll see the world like...little children, brand new...*(She describes the world so vividly that they are lost in it.)* The sky will be so blue, and the leaves so green and making the sound like the ocean...ssh...ssh...

GEORGE: *tâpwê?*

ERNESTINE: That's what *kôhkominaw* said...and I believe her... we have to believe her...

*(*GEORGE *goes outside with* GENEVIEVE.*)*

Scene IX

*(*GEORGE *and* GENEVIEVE *are sitting in a city park.)*

GEORGE: It's my fault that the storm came, a punishment for what I did. I'm a traitor, having the *môniyâs* come to see them like animals in a cage, Indians in the ghetto...making fools out of our people.... Oh shit, look around us, no stone stands unturned...and here I was trying to sell our people. Sin, I'm a sinner. *(He takes a handful of dirt and pours some on his head.)* I'll have to wander the earth for all the days of my life, like Cain with a mark on my head, and all the people will turn to me and say, *wiya ana kâ-kakwê-atâwâkêt nêhiyawa....* This is what they will say, and there'll be no place for me to hide...*(He pours some more dirt on his head and bangs the earth.) nikitimâkisin, nikitimâkisin.*

GENEVIEVE: There's nothing wrong with what you did. You tried to show your relatives their beauty where they don't see any sometimes...in their auntie's smile, their uncle's laugh...that's all you did and that was good.

GEORGE: No, no, I made fools of them, the folks from Fort Lauderdale would've laughed and talked about us down in Florida...

GENEVIEVE: No don't regret anything, think about it as if you learned something. Our people would've learned something, too. Your mother did. She wouldn't let anybody come and look at her like in a zoo. If your mom really did say yes, then it would have been something to cry about. Once our women get weak, then there goes our people, into the history books.... No, don't regret anything. Me, I don't regret nothing. I just laugh or cry about it, then go on. If I regretted all the things I've done in my life I'd be doing penance from here to old age.... You wouldn't believe some of the things I've done, things I've said, enough to make your ears curl.... Oh God, some of the guys I've gone out with, now that's something to cry about, *ca...(Laughs.)*...hey, come on, you did good. It was crazy, that's why I helped you. And when you do crazy things, that's when the spirits really stop to look.... See, look, it's a new day after the storm. See our people are still laughing, they're happy and they're not angry...

(They look at the street. GEORGE sees someone approaching.)

GEORGE: Genevieve, look.... Who's that?

GENEVIEVE: Maybe he heard about what you did.

(GEORGE looks closer. It is an old man dressed in the old style, a grey hat over a colourful kerchief and wearing a dark hat.)

GEORGE: I haven't seen an old man like that in years, last time when I was just a kid on the reserve.

GENEVIEVE: He looks like my *mosôm,* let's go talk to him.

(He stops her.)

GEORGE: *kiya.*

(They both look and see an old man. He finds a spot and very carefully cleans it of debris. He turns to GEORGE and GENEVIEVE.)

OLD MAN: *nôsisimak*...now we're going to call the buffalo...

(With his stick, he draws a buffalo in the ground. He says some words which are indistinguishable. Thousands of buffalo come thundering from the north. The whole horizon is filled with them and the ground shakes. They thunder close and stop. A lone, brave buffalo comes forward. She rolls in the dirt, and when she stands, she is human, a woman. She is walking.... It's ERNESTINE.)

ERNESTINE: The buffalo, we suffered for you and gave our lives so you could live on this wonderful earth.... Look, *miywâsin,* eh? On this beautiful plain where there is no fence, where we run and run...*kayâs,* our flesh and blood was your food, our bones were your weapons and tools, our skin your tents and blankets...we showed you how to lay down your life for all your relatives, and there is no act greater than that...The deed of a warrior. Today, I wanted to tell you that I don't know if our hearts can take being silent...

(She turns and walks back. She rolls in the dirt, and when she stands she is a buffalo and she joins the herd. The old man starts to erase the drawing, and the buffalo thunder away and disappear from where they came, the empty horizon.)

Scene X

(GEORGE and GENEVIEVE go to GRANNY's room.)

GEORGE: *tânisi âtawiya*

GRANNY: Not bad, *kiya?*

GEORGE: Not bad.

GRANNY: I bet I know who your granny was...Constance Lariviere.

GENEVIEVE: Yeah, she was.

GRANNY: You look like her, she's the one who taught me to smoke and chew snuff and spit like this. *(She feigns a spit.) ca, ay-apik.* You two look good with each other.... They used to say to people who didn't have anybody, this goes for bachelors, spinsters, fools, crazy ones. "Don't worry, *ohcitaw ka-nakiskawâw awiyak, kîci-âyiwâkipayîs...* you're bound to meet someone, a fellow leftover like yourself, so take heart."

(The two look at each other shyly.)

GEORGE: *nôhkom, ê-kî-pawâtamâhk.* This buffalo came to us and when she came close, she rolled on the ground and she became a woman. She told us about laying down our lives for all our relatives. What does this mean?

GRANNY: *mâmaskâc...*I was just a young girl and I was going home from day school run by the priest. I heard him talk about Good and Evil. About how before we were saved by Jesus, we had been living in the house of Satan, who was like our father, and that now we were saved. *mâka* to me this was a bunch of *mêyi,* I knew this wasn't true, because there was many good people living on the reserve. While I was walking home, I stopped at the house of this old woman living way back in the bush. I called...*nôhkom*...and she came out...opening her door slowly...she was about this high, no teeth, and she was smiling...we visited for awhile and I told her what I had heard that day. She sat there for awhile before she said anything...*piyis,* she said...*nôsisim, kayâs* our old people didn't use words like Good and Evil, Satan...*konita,* they just tried to scare us, *namôya.* All the old people used to say was for us to be kind with each other...*ka-manâcihacik kîci-ayisiyinîmak,* be kind to your fellow human beings. All these years that I am alive the voice I hear the strongest is the voice of this little old woman who told me *ka-manâcihacik kîci-ayisiyinîmak.* This is what it means to lay down your life for all your relatives. Yes, we start from there and there is no Hell, Good and Evil, only the suffering and the happiness you give in your life to another human being, and to the earth our mother...

BONIFACE: All your answers are out there.

Guide to the Pronunciation of Cree Dialogue in

All My Relatives

Jean L. Okimâsis and Arok Wolvengrey

In the following list of the Cree vocabulary found in *All My Relatives*, an approximate English pronunciation is given for each word, phrase, or sentence, along with a translation. The pronunciation is broken into syllables with primary stress indicated in FULL CAPS, while secondary stress is given in SMALL CAPS. An example of this is as follows:

maskisin .... *"shoe, moccasin"*
[MUSS kis SIN]

The Cree word *maskisin,* "shoe, moccasin," thus follows the same stress pattern as the English word "medicine," with primary stress on the first syllable, and a small amount of secondary stress on the final syllable.

Act One – Scene I

p.25 **ôta** .... *"here"*
[oh TUH]
âskaw mâna .... *"from time to time"*
[aas COW maa NUH]
êkwa .... *"now"*
[ay KWUH]
niwanikiskisin .... *"I forget"*
[ni WUN nik KISS kis SIN]

p. 25 **tânitê ê-ayâyan?** . . . . *"where are you?"*
[TAAN tay ay HI yaa YUN]
tânitê ôma ê-ayâyan? . . . . *"where are you?"*
[taan TAY oh MUH ay HI yaa YUN]

p. 26 **yaw, awiyak pê-itohtêw** . . . . *"you, someone is coming"*
[YOW UH we yuk PAY toeh TAYOO]
(Boniface) cî ana? . . . . *"Is that (Boniface)?"*
[...TSEE uh NUH]
tâpwê? . . . . *"really?"*
[taa PWAY]
âsay mîna êtikwê . . . . *"already, I guess,"*
[aas SIGH mean NAY tik KWAY]
tâpwê cî? . . . . *"really?"*
[taa PWAY tsee]

p. 27 **cîpayak** . . . . *"ghosts"*
[TSEE pie YUK]
tâpwê . . . . *"really!"*
[taa PWAY]
nôsisim, âstam . . . . *"Grandchild, come here."*
[NOHS sim aas STUM]
nôsisim, kikî-wâpamâwak cî . . . . *"Grandchild, did you see them?"*
[NOHS sim kik KEE waap PUM maaw WUK tsee]
pêyak . . . . *"one"*
[pay YUK]
ê-kikiskawât? . . . . *"it was wearing..."*
[ay kik KISS kuh WAAT]
ôma . . . . *"it is that..."*
[oh MUH]
aspin . . . . *"since"*
[us SPIN]
âta . . . . *"although"*
[aa TUH]
mwâc . . . . *"no"*
[mwaats]
nititêyihtên . . . . *"I think"*
[nit TAY yih TAYN]
mâka . . . . *"but"*
[maa GUH]
hâw, kiyâm nôsisim . . . . *"Okay, nevermind grandchild."*
[HOW kee YAAM NOHS sim]

p.27 **môy kakêtihk nisîpâpêkinên** (thank you) . . . . *"I really (thank you) a great deal."*
[moee KAY teehk nis SEE paah PAY kin NAYN]
{lit: "not a little do I stretch out my (thank you)"}

p.28 **mâna** . . . . *"usually"*
[maa NUH]

pakahkam . . . . *"I guess"*
[puk KAAH kum]

nc!, nîsta . . . . *"(Expression of disgust), me too"*
[NCH! nees TUH]

tânêhki? . . . . *"why?"*
[TAAN nayh KI]

osâm . . . . *"because/for"*
[oh SAAM]

tâpiskôc . . . . *"like/as if"*
[TAAP skohts]

âskaw mâna . . . . *"from time to time"*
[aas COW maa NUH]

kî-itwêwak mâna . . . . *"they used to say"*
[kee IT tway WUK maa NUH]

tânêhki? . . . . *"why?"*
[TAAN nayh KI]

p.29 **tâpiskôc mâna** . . . . *"it seems"*
[TAAP SKOHTS maa NUH]

osâm mâna nama kîkway . . . . . *"for there's usually nothing at all"*
[oh SAAM maa nuh num MUH kee GWHY]

môya êkwa . . . . *"not now"*
[moy YAY gwuh]

tâh-tâpwê . . . . *"it's true"*
[TAAH taap PWAY]

êkwa . . . . *"now"*
[ay GWUH]

ê-kitimâkisiyahk . . . . *"we are pitiful"*
[ay KIT tim maa KISS see YUHK]

nôhkom . . . . *"Grandma"*
[NOH koom]

nôsisimak . . . . *"Grandchildren"*
[nohs SIS smuk]

tâpwê . . . . *"really"*
[taa PWAY]

p.29 **mâka** . . . . *"but"*
[maa GUH]
p.30 **kimosômipaninawak** . . . . *"our grandfathers"*
[KIM mo SOHM pun NIN nuh WUK]
nôhkom mâna . . . . *"my grandmother, usually"*
[noh KOOM maa NUH]
mâmaskâc . . . . *"amazing"*
[MAAM muss KAATS]
tânitê êtikwê ê-itâpâsot? . . . *"I wonder where she was travelling?"*
[taan TAY tik kway ay TAAP paa SOOT] {repeated twice}
piyis . . . . *"finally"*
[pee YISS]
tâpwê mâka . . . . *"but it's true"*
[taa PWAY maa GUH]
kâwi ôta . . . . *"back to here"*
[cow WIH oh TUH]

Scene II

p.31 **wahwâ** . . . . *"oh my!"*
[wuh WAA]
kîkwây mâka ê-kaskikwâtaman? . . . . *"What are you sewing?"*
[kee GWHY maa guh ay KUS kik KWAA tuh MUN]
miywâsin . . . . *"good"*
[MEE waa SIN]
piyâhtik . . . . *"watch out/careful"*
[PEE yaah TIK] . . . .
kikiskêyihtên cî tânêhki ohci? . . . . *"do you know why?"*
[kik kiss KAY yih TAYN tsee TAAN nayhk OH tsih]
p.32 **wîhtikow** . . . . *"cannibal monster"*
[WEEH tik koe]
wîhtikow . . . . *"cannibal monster"*
[WEEH tik koe] {repeated six times}
ôta ka-pê-icâscamohcêsin
. . . . *"You'll come walking here in a funny little way*
[oh TUH kuh pay TSAAS tsum MOH tsay SIN]
sîkosâkanak . . . . *"cracklings"*
[SEE koe SAA gun NUK] . . . .
ca . . . . *"(expression of disgust or joking)"*
[tsuh]

p.33 **'skanak, kîminîcâkan** . . . . *"bitch! bastard!"*
[skun NUK KEE min NEE tsaa GUN]
kiyâpic . . . . *"still"*
[KEE yaa PITS]
takopayiki . . . . *"when it arrives"*
[TUK ko PIE yik KIH]
konita . . . . *"for nothing"*
[CONE tuh]
niwâhkômâkanitik . . . . *"hey, my relatives"*
[ni WAAH koe maa GUN nit TIK]
ôma . . . . *"this"*
[oh MUH]
nc!, î, ana . . . . *"(expression of disgust), aww, that one"*
[NCH! EE uh NUH]

p.34 **môy kakêtihk** . . . . *"a great deal"*
[MOEE kay tihk]
mêskanâhk ana . . . . *"on the road, that one"*
[MACE kun NAAHK uh NUH]
mâka . . . . *"but"*
[maa GUH]
tânêhki? . . . . *"why?"*
[TAAN nayh kih]
êkot ôhci . . . . *"from there..."*
[AY kot OH tsi]
(headache) k-âyât . . . . *"she has (a headache)"*
[...KAA yaat]
ay-api . . . . *"sit down"*
[EYE yuh PIH]
wahwâ . . . . *"wow"*
[wuh WAA]
kayâs . . . . *"long ago"*
[kie YAAS]
âstam . . . . *"come here"*
[aas STUM]
nah, nîcimos, ka-sîwahcikân
. . . . *"Take it, sweetheart, you'll eat something sweet."*
[NUH NEE tsim MOOSE KUH see WUHT tsig GAAN]

p.35 **êkosi** . . . . *"Okay, that's it"*
[AY koe sih]

p.35 **nôhkom** . . . . *"Grandma"*
[NOH koom]

Scene III

p.36 **ayapâcinâsihk nicihcîkinêspikêkanênison**
. . . . *"I'm scratching my own ribs in the hills."*
[EYE yuh paat TSIN naa seehk nit TSEEH tsee kin NACE pik KAY gun NAY nis SOON] {Cree tongue twister}

p.37 **tâpwê** . . . . *"really"*
[taa PWAY]

Scene IV

p.38 **nôhkom, tânisi** . . . . *"Grandma, hello, how are you?"*
[NOH koom TAAN sih]
tânêhki? . . . . *"why?"*
[TAAN nayh kih]
tânitê . . . . *"where?"*
[TAAN tay]

p.39 **ôma** . . . . *"this"*
[oh MUH] . . . . {repeated twice}
namôya cî kîkway ê-kiskêyihtaman?
. . . . *"Don't you know anything?"*
[num MOEE TSEE kee GWHY AY kis KAYHT tum MUN]
wîhtikowak . . . . *"cannibal monsters"*
[weeh TIK koe WUK]
pitawê . . . . *"?"*
[PEE tuh WAY]
kâ-kî-itiht . . . . *"as he was called"*
[kaa KEE it TEEHT]
êkwa awa nôhkom . . . . *"and this one my grandmother"*
[ay GWAAW WUH nooh KOOM]

p.40 **nîsta** . . . . *"me, too"*
[nees TUH]
kiwâpamâw cî awa? . . . . *"Do you see this one?"*
[kih WAA pum MAAW TSEE uh WUH]
êkwa . . . . *"and"*
[ay GWUH]

p.40 **tânêhki?** . . . . *"why?"*
[TAAN nayh kih]

p.41 **cêskwa, cêskwa** . . . . *"wait, wait"*
[chase KWUH, chase KWUH]

sâsay cî, wahwâhay . . . . *"already? oh my"*
[saa SIGH tsee wuh waa HI]

Scene V

p.42 **êkwa** . . . . *"now"*
[ay GWUH]

Scene VII

p.43 **kîkwây ê-tôtamân** . . . . *"what do I do?"*
[kee GWHY ay TOTE tum MAAN]

p.44 **nôsisim** . . . . *"Grandchild"*
[NOHS sim]

Scene VIII

p.44 **pihêw** . . . . *"prairie chicken" (used as a name)*
[pih HAYOO]

mônicâskwêw (daughter) cî? . . . *"Bachelor-woman's daughter?"*
[MOAN tsaas KWAYOO (daw TER) TSEE]

kôkom's . . . . *"your grandmother's"*
[KOE koomz]

pihêw . . . . *"prairie chicken" (used as a name)*
[pih HAYOO]

p.45 **awas** . . . . *"go on, go away"*
[uh WUSS] {repeated three times}

iskwêsip . . . . *"lady duck" (used as a name)*
[ISS kway SIP]

pikw îtê ê-pâstêk . . . . *"it's dry everywhere"*
[poke WEE tay AY paas TAYK]

tâpwê . . . . *"it's true"*
[taa PWAY]

p.46 **nc!** . . . . *"(expression of disgust)"*
[INCH]

p.46 **awas, niyâ** . . . . *"go away, go on"*
[uh WUSS nee YAA]

p.47 **nc!** . . . . *(expression of disgust)*
[INCH]

kôkom . . . . *"(your) grandmother"*
[KOH koom]

tâpwê . . . . *"it's true"*
[taa PWAY]

Scene IX

p.48 **ispîhk ê-kî-wawêsîyân** . . . . *"when I was prepared"*
[iss PEEHK ay KEE wuh WAY see YAAN]

nôhkom mâna . . . . *"my grandmother, usually,..."*
[noh KOOM maa nuh]

tânitahto kîsikâw ôta kâ-papêhowân?
. . . . *"How many days will I wait?"*
[taan TUH toe KEE sik COW oh TUH kaa puh PAY hoe WAAN]

tânitahto askiy ôta kâ-papêhowân?
. . . . *"How many years will I wait?"*
[taan TUH twuss KEE oh TUH kaa puh PAY hoe WAAN]

piyis nikihtimêyihtên ka-pêyakowân, ...
. . . . *"At last, I'm tired of being alone."*
[pee YISS nik KEEH tim MAY yih TAYN kuh pay YUK koe WAAN]

nikihtimêyihtên ka-kaskêyihtamân... *"I'm tired of being lonely."*
[nik KEEH tim MAY yih TAYN kuh KUSS kay YIHT tum MAAN]

p49 **awas êkosi,** . . . . *"go on, it's done"*
[uh WUSS AY koe sih]

p.50 **wâ** . . . . *"well,"*
[waa]

kwêyask osihtâ . . . . *"make it straight"*
[kway YUSK OH seeh TAA]

(arrow) osihtâ . . . . *"make an arrow"*
[...OH seeh TAA]

p.51 **kîcimos** . . . . *"sweetheart"*
[KEE tsim MOOS]

p.52 **kayâs** . . . . *"long ago"*
[kie YAAS]

p.52 **kiya ôma kâ-sâkihitân** . . . . *"You're the one I love."*
[KEE yoh MUH KAA saa KIH hit TAAN]
namôy wihkâc na-sipwêhtân . . . . *"I'll never leave."*
[num MOEE weeh KAATS nuh SIP pwayh TAAN]
niwâpikwaniy, niwâpikwaniy . . . . *"my flower, my flower"*
[nih waa PIG gwun NEE nih waa PIG gwun NEE]

Scene XI

p.55 **awas wîn-atim** . . . . *"go on, dirty dog"*
[uh WUSS WEE nut TIM]
yîkatêhtê . . . . *"move aside"*
[yii KUT tayh TAY]
nôhkom . . . . *"Grandmother"*
[noh KOOM]
na, pihêw . . . . *"well, Pihêw"*
[NUH pih HAYOO]
cah . . . . *"expression of disgust"*
[tsuh]
hâm mâka kîsta . . . . *"all right, now you too"*
[haam maa guh keese tuh]
wîcihtâso . . . . *"help out"*
[wee TSEEH taa SO]
p.56 **niyâ** . . . . *"go on"*
[nee YAA]
kiyipa . . . . *"quickly"*
[KEE yi PUH]
nôhtâ . . . . *"Father"*
[noh TAA]

Act Two – Scene I

p.57 **awas** . . . . *"go on"*
[uh WUSS]
tânêhki? . . . . *"why?"*
[TAAN nayh kih]

Scene II

p.58 **nôhkom** . . . . *"Grandmother"*
[noh KOOM]
namôya, namôya, pitamâ . . . . *"no, no, for now"*
[num MOEE yuh num MOEE YUH PIT TUM maa]
apik . . . . *"sit!"*
[up PIK]
nôsisim . . . . *"Grandchild"*
[NOHS sim]
p.59 **kiyâm** . . . . *"nevermind"*
[kee YAAM]
nêhiyaw ê-kî-miyikowisit cistêmâs
. . . . *"The Cree were given tobacco."*
[NAY he YOW ay kee MEE yi KOE sit TSIS tay MAAS]
wiya . . . . *"Him"*
[we YUH] {repeated twice}
âhkamêyimok . . . . *"Persevere!"*
[aah kum MAY yim mook]
kayâs . . . . *"long ago"*
[kie YAAS]
ê-mistakêyimisocik . . . . *"They thought a lot of themselves."*
[ay MISS tuk KAY yim MISS so TSIK]
p.60 **môy nikiskêyihtên** . . . . *"I don't know."*
[MOEE nik kiss KAY yih TAYN]
ahâw . . . . *"yes!/okay"*
[uh HOW]
kiya mâka, tânisi . . . . *"And you, how are you?"*
[KEE yuh MAA guh TAAN sih]
ho, kîkwâya? . . . . *"oh, what (things)?"*
[hoe KEE gwhy yuh]
kîkwây mâka . . . . *"what's that?"*
[kee GWHY maa GUH]
tâpwê cî? . . . . *"really!?"*
[taap PWAY tsee]
p.61 **sîpiy** . . . . *"river"*
[see PEE]
miywâsin . . . . *"it's good"*
[MEE waa SIN]
cî? . . . . *"right?"*
[tsee]

Scene III

p.62 **âhkamêyimok** . . . . *"Persevere!"*
[AAH kum MAY yim MOOK]
p.63 **iskonikanak** . . . . *"leftovers"*
[iss koe NIG gun nuk]
kôhkominaw . . . . *"our grandmother"*
[koeh KOOM min NOW]
p.64 **kôkom** . . . . *"grandma"*
[KOE kum]
tânisi . . . . *"hello"*
[TAAN sih]
ca . . . . *"(joking expression)"*
[chuh]
wâ . . . . *"wow"*
[waa]
p.65 **kî-itwêwak mâna** . . . . *"They call usually"*
[kee IT tway WUK MAA NUH]

Scene IV

ê-minihkwêyahk . . . . *"as we're drinking"*
[AY min NEEH kway YUHK]
p.66 **okîsikowak** . . . . *"the angels"*
[oh kee SIK koe WUK]
kikanawâpamikonawak . . . . *"(they) look out for us"*
[kik KUN nuh WAA pum mik KOE now WUK]
ê-kitimâkisiyahk . . . . *"we're pitiful"*
[ay KIT im maa KISS see YUHK]
kîkwây kê-itwêwak? . . . . *"what would they say?"*
[kee GWHY KAY tway WUK]
kikitimâkisinânaw . . . . *"we're pitiful"*
[kik KIT tim MAA kiss SIN naa NOW]

Scene V

p.68 **êtikwê** . . . . *"I guess"*
[AY tik KWAY]
p.69 **waniskâ** . . . . *"get up"*
[WUN nis SKAA]

p.69 **awas, kiyipa** . . . . *"go on, quickly"*
[uh WUSS KEE yip PUH]
piyis . . . . *"finally"*
[pee YISS]
p.70 **tânisi niwâhkômâkanitik** . . . . *"Greetings my relatives."*
[TAAN sih nihWAAHK koe maa GUN nit TIK]
anohc niminihkwân . . . . *"today I drink"*
[un NOHTS nim MIN neeh KWAAN]
kâya nânitaw itêyihta . . . . *"think nothing of it"*
[kaa yuh NAAN tow it TAY yih TUH]
namôy kihtwâm nika-minihkwân . . . *"I'll never drink again."*
[num MOEE keeh TWAAM nik kuh MIN neeh KWAAN]
tâpwê . . . . *"it's true"*
[taa PWAY]
môy kihtwâm . . . . *"not again"*
[MOEE keeh TWAAM]
atimociskak . . . . *"dog's asses"*
[UT tim MOO tsis KUK]
tânêhki . . . . *"why"*
[TAAN nayh KIH]
p.71 **hâm mâka** . . . . *"okay, on with it"*
[HAAM maa GUH]
ânakacâ . . . . *"oh, for goodness sake"*
[aa NUK kut TSAA]

Scene VI

p.72 **êkwa** . . . . *"now"*
[ay GWUH]

Scene VIII

p.74 **êkwa** . . . . *"now"*
[ay GWUH]
p.75 **cwâ** . . . . *"(expression of disbelief)"*
[CHAAW]
p.77 **âmî...âmî...** . . . . *"oh dear, oh dear"*
[aa MEE aa MEE]
tâpwê? . . . . *"really?"*
[taa pway]

p.77 **kôhkominaw** . . . . *"our grandmother"*
[koeh KOOM min NOW]
môniyâs . . . . *"Whiteman"*
[MOAN nee YAAS]

p.78 **wiya ana kâ-kakwê-atâwâkêt nêhiyawa...**
. . . . *"That's the one who tried to sell the Crees."*
[wee YAA nuh KAA kuk KWAY ut TAAW waa KAYT nay HE yow WUH]
nikitimâkisin, nikitimâkisin . . . . *"I'm pitiful, I'm pitiful"*
[nik KIT tim MAA kiss SIN nik KIT tim MAA kiss SIN]
ca . . . . *"(expression of joking)"*
[chuh]

p.79 **mosôm** . . . . *"grandpa"*
[MOE shoom]
kiya . . . . *"you"*
[kee YUH]
nôsisimak . . . . *"Grandchildren"*
[noh SIS sim MUK]
miywâsin . . . . *"it's good"*
[MEE waa SIN]
kayâs . . . . *"long ago"*
[kie YAAS]

Scene X

p.80 **tânisi âtawiya** . . . . *"are you anyway"*
[TAAN saa TAO wee YUH]
kiya? . . . . *"you?"*
[kee YUH]
ca, ay-apik . . . . *"ach, sit!"*
[CHUH EYE up PIK]
ohcitaw ka-nakiskawâw awiyak
. . . . *"You'll certainly meet someone."*
[OH tsit TAO kuh nuk KISS kow WOW OW we YUK]
kîci-âyiwâkipayîs . . . . *"your fellow leftover"*
[KEE tsih EYE yih waa KIP pie YEESE]
nôhkom, ê-kî-pawâtamâhk . . . *"Grandmother, we had a dream"*
[NOH koom ay KEE pow WAA tum MAAHK]
mâmaskâc . . . . *"amazing"*
[MAA mus KAATS]
mâka . . . . *"but"*
[maa GUH]

p.80 **mêyi** . . . . *"dung/shit"*
[may YIH]

p.81 **nôhkom** . . . . *"grandma"*
[NOH koom]

piyis . . . . *"finally"*
[pee YIS]

nôsisim, kayâs . . . . *"Grandchild, long ago"*
[NOH sim kie YAAS]

konita . . . . *"for nothing"*
[CONE tuh]

namôya . . . . *"no"*
[num MOEE yuh]

ka-manâcihacik kîci-ayisiyinîmak
. . . . *"you must be respectful of your fellow human beings"*
[KUH mun naa TSIH hut TSIK keet TSIGH yis see YIN nee MUK]
{repeated twice}

ANTIGONE

Deanne Kasokeo

This play is dedicated to my father, Daryl Kasokeo, for giving me the inspiration to succeed.

characters

ANTIGONE – *Native Woman*

CHIEF CREON – *Native Chief (Uncle of Antigone)*

ISMENE – *Antigone's sister*

COUNCILLOR – *Chief's right hand person*

HAEMON – *Chief's son*

EURYDICE – *Chief's wife*

PANOON – *Messenger*

TIRESIAS – *A blind prophet*

Band Members

BUDDY – *Elder*

EDWARD

ANSTON

BEATRICE – *Elder*

MARTA

CONSTABLE BOUCHER

CHORUS – *Ancestral spirits*

Act I – Scene I

(Setting: Outside a band hall on a Native reserve. It is semi-dark, we can see smoke and hear the cracklings of fire. CHORUS *enters. There is the illusion of fire and smoke as grass fires burn in the distance...)*

CHORUS: *(Listening and smelling.)*

My people, listen. Do you hear?
The cracklings in the distance bring forth fear.
They are thunderous, feel the trees dying,
  the grass melting,
Spreading rapidly and taking all existence.
The smoke fills the air in a thick smog
  and the flames devour all in sight.
Do you see it?
Look deep into your souls
  and feel your eyes burning within you.
Oh, so full of truth and the righteousness you behold,
Blinded by common routine,
You suffer the consequences of others,
Products of oppression,
To abide by other men's laws.
Go! Go find the wisdom you seek
For you and your sisters and brothers.
You are not feeble – the answers lie within you.
The time is near for you to learn of fate
Creeping up in distant crimes.
The mere hope of tragedy is the mere hope
  of justice for everyone.

*(*CHORUS *fades away and slowly a light illuminates a band meeting.)*

(Setting: A band meeting is taking place in the band hall. The band hall is old, small, and run down. The CHIEF *and Council are sitting at tables in front of the membership.)*

CHIEF: Before we get started with the agenda, I'd like to address the situation of the fire. Now there is no need to get alarmed, it is just a grass fire across the river and it's going to be controlled *(pauses)* ah...very soon and we don't think it will cross the river.

(Band member stands up.)

EDWARD: What do you mean, it will be controlled soon? And how do you know it won't cross the river? It has before. Remember last year's grass fire? It darned near burnt the store and a few houses down. People should be responsible for their fires, these grass fires burn for days before something is done about it. It's like we just sit back and say *(Mimicking)* "Hey, the fire is kinda out of control...I think we better put it out."

ANSTON: There should be some procedure or rule where people should look after their grass fires instead of having grass fire "haydays" every spring and getting everybody alarmed for something that can be regulated.

CHIEF: Well, like I said, we have it under control. *(Sure of himself.).* We have the water truck out there along with the caterpillar and a few band members are helping out.

ANSTON: *(Blurts out.)* Where's the fire truck anyway?

CHIEF: Maybe one of the councillors could take the floor to answer that. *(He looks at his councillors and then he seats himself.)*

(COUNCILLOR stands up.)

COUNCILLOR: *(Sighs.)* Well, the tires were stolen awhile back and it will be receiving new tires once the funding is available so we can take it out of the garage.

ANSTON: *(Stands up.)* I thought we just got the new funding? By the time it's brought over here the grass fire season will be over. I don't believe this.

EDWARD: Oh yeah! How come I didn't get new plumbing in my house? I've been asking for the past year. Pretty soon my toilet won't work no more and I'll have to resort to an outhouse. You guys *(Pointing at the* CHIEF.*)* keep telling me "next month" but that time never comes and soon I will show *you* where my toilet is because you're so full of shit. *(Sits down.)*

(Band members gasping and whispering.)

CHIEF: Now! Now! Can we have some order here, we don't need to speak this way. This is a meeting. I am sure we can all speak appropriately. *(Pauses.)* Thank you. The fire is going to be put out and that concludes the issue. Now we can go with the agenda. First we will give a rundown on each portfolio of the councillors and then we will have questions and concerns answered. Okay. First we'll have our first councillor speaking on the new developments in his office.

COUNCILLLOR: *(Stands up and speaks with a cheery voice.): tânisi!* All my relations. I will speak on the housing situation first of all – Edward, just after the new fiscal year we received our new monies and we are going to be doing renovations for four houses and we will build three new houses. And to add to your concern for plumbing...we have taken your application into consideration and you should be getting your plumbing this year.

EDWARD: *(Stands up and interrupts, excited.)* Do you think you can throw in one of those pink toilet seats? My old lady likes pink.

CHIEF: No, we don't throw in those kinds of luxuries, that would be too much money. Indian Affairs doesn't give us funding for things like that, and it's not in our budget.

EDWARD: *cwâ!* Why?

CHIEF: What for?

EDWARD: Wellll! The new fiscal year was just this month. Wasn't it? *(Nodding his head.)* We have lots of money. All you guys sitting up there drive nice new vehicles almost every year. All you do is drive around anyway; you don't do nothing but show off your new trucks at the store...

COUNCILLOR: *(Interrupts)* All Right! Like I said, we are going to do four minor house renovations and build three new houses.

MARTA: How come there will be only three new houses? Usually we'd have six new houses and renovations.

COUNCILLOR: *(Clears his throat.)* Well, the band is trying to recover from a minor deficit *(Under his breath.)* from last year and we only have enough monies to build three houses this year. But this year we will have four small minor house renovations, so I guess that will offset the difference *(Pauses.)* kind of. By next year the deficit should be diminished.

MARTA: Are you saying the deficit may not be recovered by the new year or what? How can we have such a deficit? What are the band monies being spent on? There is nothing to show for it. Are the band monies mismanaged or what? I think we should know about these things.

COUNCILLOR: *(Hesitantly.)* No. No. It's nothing like that. Right now we don't know where or when the cutbacks will take place. We are really trying hard to make things fair around here, and help out everybody as much as possible. It is good that we have this opportunity to listen to your concerns and that we have this type of communication.

ANSTON: Hey, how come we didn't get KFC for dinner before the band meeting? We always get KFC before the meeting. *(Pauses, waiting for answer.)* Or is it after the band meeting?

CHIEF: People, can we please stick to the agenda? And NO, there is no KFC on the agenda today.

(Some people get up and leave.)

Scene II

(Setting: A*NTIGONE'S house.)*

ANTIGONE: When will we ever find justice Ismene? Polynices' body is waiting in some funeral home while he has nowhere to be buried. Our poor brother. Can't Chief Creon see this is where he belongs? Our home, the reserve! It brings me sorrow knowing that our own people can create so much injustice. He is nothing without the membership. We put him there! We must abide by his superficial laws because if we don't, we have no rights here. Even the reserve dogs have more status here. I am tired of it all. I will no longer abide by his rule or law, no more! I have nothing to lose. *(She pauses and listens.)* Ismene, do you hear that? I feel for Polynices, his spirit weeps. *(Takes a deep breath.)* My heart is heavy. His spirit needs to find peace here in his rightful burial place.

ISMENE: Oh, Antigone, I want to help you, and I know what you are saying is true. But our family no longer holds the power on this reserve. In Creon's mind, he is right and he holds the power.

ANTIGONE: This is our home too – we have rights like everybody else. We have to take into our own hands what is just. His wake isn't even right. Our poor brother is suffering. Ismene, we only have two more days until burial. You know that the dead have to be buried within four days or their spirit will wander forever in this world, trapped. As his sisters, we cannot let this happen.

ISMENE: I know, but look at what the Chief did to our brother. Do you want to suffer the same consequences? I know it's wrong to bury him in town, away from his ancestors, away from where our mother, Jocasta, buried his umbilical cord, but what can we do? He'll be buried, Antigone. I love our brother, too. For all we know, the Chief will banish us if we bring his body home. Our family has been through so much, and through all of this turmoil, Chief Creon gloats as we slowly die. Creon hated our father, that is the root of his hatred for us...all we have is each other now. We must protect ourselves.

ANTIGONE: All right, Ismene. I respect your position, but I am prepared to face any consequences brought upon me. I am going to bring Polynices home. His spirit has been lost since he was BCR'd* from the reserve, and still it lingers. I must help him. He is our mother's child...sister, look into my eyes and tell me that you would not do the same for me.

ISMENE: I am afraid of the power of their laws –

ANTIGONE: He does not control the laws of the dead. Listen – right now they are having a band meeting at the hall. Will you come with me? I am going to approach Chief and council about having Polynices buried here.

ISMENE: Antigone, I admire your strength. I am weak and I cannot bear what may happen to you. Our brother died a horrible death after he was banished from here. You know them, in their eyes we are nothing. They won't take us seriously, we are women.

ANTIGONE: They can't say no in front of the people. Rightfully, he belongs here and I want them to see that this is a law they can't manipulate. These unwritten laws are here eternally.

ISMENE: (Hesistant.) Okay, I will go with you, but I will not speak for you.

ANTIGONE: I will speak for our brother. The only loyalty here is to our family, and no one else. Thank you, Ismene, for coming with me. You don't have to speak a word.

(They start to walk out. ISMENE stops ANTIGONE.)

ISMENE: All I have is my sister – please be careful.

---

* *BCR: Band Council Resolution*

Scene III

(Setting: Band hall, where a band meeting is in progress. ANTIGONE *and* ISMENE *enter the hall. People gasp and stare.* CHIEF *and council do not see them yet.)*

COUNCILLOR: Anyway, that is how the operation of the garbage and sewer system will take place. We can only pick garbage up once every two weeks now, so you'll have to hang on to your garbage awhile longer or transport it yourselves. The sewage system will also be getting cut back.

BUDDY (ELDER): *(Interrupts) cwâ!* What do you mean? The sewer is always backed up...

COUNCILLOR: Excuse me, in terms of water, we have not decided upon the status of that yet, but most likely, we will have to cut back on that also.

BUDDY: Well, what are us old people supposed to do if you cut back on the water? We don't have wells or the manpower to get our own water or even transport our own garbage.

COUNCILLOR: We understand that, but we just don't have all the answers right now. We will find another alternative for the elders, maybe. *êkosi!* Now we leave the floor open for any questions.

CHIEF: For a few minutes!

BEATRICE (ELDER): *(She stands up holding her cane.)* I'd just like to say, I am an urban band member and, like other urban band members, I am ready to move home. I've been asking for a house for the past twelve years. How long does it take to get a house? And why don't you consider the old people? We are getting tired and we want to move home. This is our home, too, we belong. We had to leave the reserve to get good jobs and to support our families. Here at the reserve there is so few jobs, and only certain people and families get ahead. I am here before you in person asking for a house. How long can you keep telling an old person "no"? You don't know how it is to live in the city where the government doesn't take care of you. My moccasins are old and they are tired of walking. I want to come home where my ancestors and relatives are in spirit, where one day I will join them.

ANOTHER ELDER: *hay hay!*

BEATRICE: Tank-you.

CHIEF: Well, Beatrice...we appreciate your input. But, nobody can tell me how to run my band. I sit here as the Chief, and looking after the reserve is like running a business. I am a businessman. I sit here to look after my people accordingly, and I must say that I have never seen any housing application from you in the time I have been Chief. I am sorry you had to leave the reserve to raise your kids elsewhere, but that is a choice you made and this is our choice to stay here. Can you imagine if all the people left? There would be no people here to secure our funding reserve and keep it running. People like us keep this place functioning. Beatrice, if you put in another application we will look at it, so send it in to the band office. If there are any more questions, please ask them now, because we are running out of time. *(He whispers to COUNCILLOR beside him.)* Have Merle make me an expense cheque. Tell her that we are going to a meeting tomorrow, then meet me at the casino this evening.

COUNCILLOR: *(Whispers back.)* Yes, Chief. I'll do that right away. I'll be there at seven.

CHIEF: No questions people? *(Some people put up their hands and CHIEF ignores them.)* Then I declare the meeting is adjourned! *(The CHIEF and Council stand up and start to leave. ANTIGONE walks up from the back of the hall; people start whispering.)*

ANTIGONE: Excuse me Chief and councilmen. I am Antigone. My mother was Jocasta. My father was Oedipus. And you, Chief, are my relative, as are many of you. I am here to address an issue as a band member.

CHIEF: Miss Antigone, if you would like to speak with us, contact my secretary at the office. This meeting is over. *(He starts walking and his men follow. Other band members walk out as well.)*

ANTIGONE: My brother, Polynices, has died and he must be buried on this reserve next to our parents within four days. I know you BCR'd him off the reserve, but, please allow him to be buried here. What harm can he do now that he is dead?

CHIEF: It's a good thing we got rid of your brother. He made the band look bad in the eyes of the public. It's a family trait, isn't it? Your father polluted the reserve with his demented form of self-government as the Chief. Look where we are now, in a deficit. His foul traits passed on to his children. Polynices was exactly like your father, dirty, and incompetent!

ANTIGONE: How dare you speak of my father and brother who have passed on and are not here to defend themselves. Polynices was a victim of your scam. You used my brother as a scapegoat and got rid of him by paying him off, and then you turn around and BCR him off the reserve forever. You killed him!

(Band members gasp and stay around to listen.)

CHIEF: Councillor, show Miss Antigone where the door is and get her out of here. We've got a meeting to go to.

(ANTIGONE is escorted out with her sister beside her.)

ANTIGONE: My brother has every right to be buried here, those are not your laws. Death requires the same burial for all.

CHIEF: Not the same for a patriot of the reserve as for a traitor. I wouldn't even consider burying a traitor to desecrate this land, and the decision I have made to not have his burial here is a good one, I must say. And yes, these are my laws, that is all that matters here. You don't pay my bills, woman. Now take her away.

ANTIGONE: Take me away? As if! Your presence here pollutes everybody and everything. This is so ridiculous. How can anyone not find this perfectly corrupt? Can I ask you one question, Chief? Are you not here to serve your people?

CHIEF: Yes, I am, and that is exactly what I am doing here. Keeping it safe from people like you, hmm, idealists.

(CHIEF walks out.)

(CHORUS comes in.)

CHORUS: Ah! We see the light,
A strong beam rising through the night.
Yes, everyone can see
That justice is as sweet as can be.
Antigone, you are the one
Who brings forth the laws of the land.
Death deserves all rites,
And it is through you, Antigone, Polynices fights.
We, the spirits, are with you.
Ah! We raise ourselves into the light
to help Polynices make his flight.

(CHORUS fades away.)

Scene IV

(Setting: The CHIEF's Oval Office)

COUNCILLOR: So did you have any luck last night?

CHIEF: No, no luck.

COUNCILLOR: I left early. You were still in the poker room...I didn't want to disturb you.

CHIEF: I sat there for at least a couple of hours and didn't win nothing. I think my luck is running out. Hmmm...I just can't seem to shake that family. Incestuous, inbred Indians. She humiliated me in front of my people. How dare she come into my meeting and speak to me about my laws. Little do these people know that under the Indian Affairs Act, I control all aspects of the reserve. I am the one that makes everything look good around here. Me, I am the authority here! Right? Councillor tell me that I am right to impose my views on my people.

COUNCILLOR: Yes, yes. Chief you are right. It's understandable to take it upon yourself to implement your laws. You know what is best for the people. Like you said, Polynices was banished from here with a BCR, and he shall stay that way, living or not! Band Council Resolutions give us the jurisdiction to enforce laws. Betrayal holds a high price.

CHIEF: *(Interrupts.)* You're right – Death is the price he pays. The mere hope of money has ruined many men. Money is power, my friend, and I have the power. I have them on my side. *(Points up.)* They are on my side the spirits. I am always protected, that's what that blind medicine woman told me after I gave her a thousand bucks. Antigone is like a little snake in the grass – just like her father and brother. That family will never change. Tell me, Councillor, you would never side with her...

COUNCILLOR: Of course not, only a fool would court banishment. Chief Creon – *(Pauses.)* I am not trying to offend you, but Polynices is your nephew and Antigone is your niece because their father is your brother.

CHIEF: Hmmmh. Yes, Einstein! But he was, I stress, my half brother. Unfortunately, my mother's other son. That does not make me family – those *kîminîcâkanak* are nothing like me, therefore they are no relation to me. I am different.

(There is a knock at the door.)

CHIEF: Come in.

(The night watchman, PANOON, comes in. He is nervous and out of breath.)

PANOON: Chief you must come quickly. Polynices has been buried...he has been given his proper rites!

CHIEF: What? What are you talking about. This just can't be. I said No! Panoon, how do you know that the body has been buried?

PANOON: Well, it's going around the reserve that it was transported secretly from the funeral home in town. It's marked with a wooden cross that says *RIP Polynices.* Actually, I seen it myself. While I was doing my duties here, I thought I'd go for a drive. I decided to check on the graveyard. There isn't even a trace of a person or persons at the grave site.

CHIEF: *RIP Polynices*...who would want to rip him?

COUNCILLOR: Rest in peace, sir.

CHIEF: *(Annoyed.)* I knew that....You want to know what I think? I think that you know too much. Are you sure it wasn't you and you're just trying to cover up your dirty deed?

PANOON: No Chief. I would never commit such a crime. That is the word going around. I told you so that I may have good fortune. Please believe me, I would never render myself against you. I voted for you. *(Sticks out his hand. He wants money.).*

CHIEF: *(Outraged.)* Get out! Go. Wait! Don't leave – I want you to take care of something.

PANOON: Yes, Chief, what is it? I will do anything to free myself of this accusation.

CHIEF: I want you to find out who buried Polynices, then come back and tell me. If you do not produce any man or woman who committed this crime, then consider yourself cut off. No more welfare for your relatives. Then maybe your sorry behind will learn that it does not pay to itch for rewards from the hand that summons. Here, I will give you this. *(Hands him money.)* If you do not bring the culprit or culprits to me, then you'll swear your money brought you pain. Now go on. I have nothing more to say to you.

(PANOON exits.)

Scene V

(Setting: CHIEF'S office. The CHIEF is sitting in his office alone.)

CHORUS: The air is thick and soon we'll see
Injustice will never set them free.
On and on we hear his laws.
Full of imbalance and nasty flaws.
He sees no wrong in his narrow mind,
Soon, soon one day he will find
That he was wrong.
"Those who disobey,"
He says, "are no longer here to stay."
He is not right, so full of nothingness.
How could he ever think anything more?
Justice is stolen by a thief.
Look towards the laws of above,
They are here forever.
The clouds are dark and swirling above,
The wind is fast and whips the land,
Destruction can be seen far.
The thunder roars and the lightning strikes!
Be ready, as there is no escaping the lashing of the rain
Purifying the earth,
Soon there will be new rebirth!
This is a sign from above:
Revenge doesn't answer all, little do you know...

(CHORUS fades.)

(CHIEF looks out his window as a storm is brewing and COUNCILLOR walks in.)

CHIEF: Look outside, Councillor, I wonder how long this storm will last? The clouds are so dark and moving fast. The wind sure has picked up. I hate these kinds of storms. We haven't had one of these for awhile. Something sure is stirring. *(Looking out the window.)*

COUNCILLOR: Yes, it is still somewhat blustery out there. There is a weather warning for our area tonight, supposed to be hail and harsh winds.

CHIEF: *(Still looking out his window.)* Weather warning, eh? Well, the rain is coming down hard. The thunder is very loud, too loud. Since I was a kid I have been scared of storms. *(Composes himself and looks at Councillor.)* This is just between you and me.

COUNCILLOR: Of course, sir. *(Pauses.)* I'm sure everything will subside shortly.

CHIEF: You know, Councillor, I really do try and make the right decisions for my people. I am never acknowledged for my hard efforts. I know that I am the Chief, that is all that matters. Without this, could I survive out in the bigger world? Out there, do you think that we could be something? Or would we be like everybody else, and have to work?

COUNCILLOR: You would be what you would make yourself out to be, Chief.

CHIEF: Hmmmmh. I guess you are right, Councillor. Where would I be without you to listen to my confessions?

(PANOON runs in and is frantic.)

Panoon: Chief, I found out who did it. I found HER! *(Pauses.)*

CHIEF: Well...

Panoon: She is guilty of the crime and she admits it. I feel relieved! I am rid of this business once and for all. Now, Chief, will you let me be free of this crime?

Chief: *(Angry.)* Who is she? And where is she?

Panoon: She is Antigone! I have her outside and she says that she is not afraid of you, and that she is ready to speak with you.

Chief: Antigone, eh? With her own hands she buried Polynices? I find that unbelievable. How do I know that she didn't have any help? Are there others to be prosecuted here? How do you know it was her and her alone, Panoon?

Panoon: *(Stutters.)* B-b-because when I went back to the gravesite, it was raining very hard and the wind was unbearable. The dust was flying, and the clouds dark and swirling above. It was as if the land was being whipped and any person in the way of it. The storm was not like any other, this was different. I looked over the hill and it was hard to see who it was. My face hurt from the rain. Then I could hear a woman's voice, a sharp piercing cry. It was really loud and she was screaming with the wind. Her back was towards me and she was on her knees with her hands in the air in front of the newly mounded grave. She was crying, but more than tears of mourning, she seemed insane. She was saying, "Yes, yes, my brother, you are free and here is your justice. Rest now, my brother." Then she fell to the ground weeping, taking the soil from the grave and wiping it on her face and arms. The rain was hitting me so hard, and then suddenly lightning hit a barren tree close to the graves. I never felt so much fear, and then she looked straight at me. She ran, and then I ran after her. She didn't stop and I kept calling her. Finally she quit running and asked me what I wanted. She knew it was you who sent for her and she's not afraid, sir. She says she did no wrong and she could care less about any consequences.

CHIEF: *(Stands up.)* Bring her in here. I will speak to Antigone myself.

(PANOON walks out and brings ANTIGONE into the CHIEF'S office.)

CHIEF: Antigone, is it true that you buried your brother, Polynices?

ANTIGONE: Of course, and I see no wrong in the burial. I don't deny it, and I am content now.

CHIEF: *(Slams his fist on his desk, then says in a stern voice.)* Were you not aware a decree had forbidden this!

ANTIGONE: Yes, Chief. I was very aware. Who wasn't? You made it very public.

CHIEF: And you still had the courage to break my laws?

ANTIGONE: What courage? This is not courage, it is simply duty. These are just your laws and maybe I'd be more cautious if they were ancestral, natural laws. I see no wrong in proper death rites. We all deserve them. Your laws could never override the natural laws, Chief! Who do you think you are? I could never allow my family to be buried elsewhere. Polynices is my mother's son and my own flesh and blood. If you think that my actions are so foolish, then let's just say that I've been accused of folly by a fool.

CHIEF: Panoon, you may leave. *(PANOON leaves.)* You evil little creature, I am not surprised that you would do something like this. Your family, you're all alike. Now you will have to pay. This is my reserve and these are my laws. Natural laws are not here. Where are they? *(Sarcastically.)* Ha, ha! I don't see them. You see, Antigone, I am a skeptic. I need to see with my own two eyes. Whatever is there, they're all on my side.

ANTIGONE: You know what, Chief? Everybody is scared to say something to you. They are afraid you may strike them with your forked tongue. It's rather sharp isn't it? I will stand up to you and defend my ground. I am not scared to open my mouth, and I will not turn my cheek when you inflict your cheap laws on me. I am proud of who I am and what I have done. Nothing could ever take this feeling of victory from me, not even you.

CHIEF: Sellout. I cannot stand a sellout who tries to glorify her crimes. There is no glory in what you have done. You are very naïve. I will have you arrested and then we will be rid of you forever. You are never to come back here.

ANTIGONE: Oh I see, that little game. You want to play again? I am no longer welcome in my own home, just like Polynices hey? Are you going to draw up another Band Council Resolution to banish me from the reserve? How tiresome. I accept my doom of death. Is there anything else you would want, Chief?

CHIEF: Nothing. I've got what I want.

ANTIGONE: So you have another murder to plan, don't you?

CHIEF: What are you talking about?

ANTIGONE: My father and my brother! Your brother and your nephew.

CHIEF: Never. Your father, Oedipus, was not my brother. I don't claim him. As for his kids you are all cursed. Your father married his own mother. My mother!

(ISMENE enters and interrupts.)

ISMENE: Chief Creon! I am guilty of the crime. Whatever consequences Antigone faces, I do as well. I am her sister, her punishment is mine too.

ANTIGONE: No, Ismene you had no part in this. You didn't help me.

ISMENE: Shame me not sister by denying me a death for honouring the dead with you.

Chief: As far as I am concerned why not kill two birds with one stone? Both of you did it.

Antigone: No. Ismene had nothing to do with this. It was all my business and no one else's. *(Faces Ismene.)* Ismene, don't share in my destruction, my death will be enough.

Ismene: And what care I for life, if I lost you?

Antigone: Ask Creon, you are dutiful to him.

Ismene: Why do you cross me so, to no good purpose?

Chief: That's enough. Redeeming is not permitted here. It doesn't matter anymore. You both will face the same prosecution.

Ismene: I will take your punishment, Uncle. But how can you banish your own son's future bride? Haemon loves her.

Chief: Why not? There are other games for him to play. To have a worthless woman for my son repulses every nerve in my body.

Antigone: Nothing could ever break the bond we have. Like any other, I was put here to love and to serve the people. You can do anything to me, Chief, but you will never rid me from Haemon. He loves me.

Chief: I've been waiting for a moment like this when I could break the engagement off. Antigone, you caused this and if it weren't for your immaturity a mountain would not have been created. This whole situation is ludicrous. *(Picks up the phone.)* Yes. Hello. This is the Chief. I have some young women here who broke a Band Council Resolution. You will come in right now and take them in. Yes, I will speak to you about this later. For now, have them wait in the jail. *(Hangs up phone.)*

Antigone: For burying my own brother? For honouring the

laws of our ancestors that say we must bury our dead within four days or their souls will eternally wander?

CHIEF: Look Woman! You chose your punishment, now take it. To break a Band Council Resolution, a BCR, is punishable by law.

(Two RCMP constables enter.)

CHIEF: These are the two young ladies. You may take the trash away.

(Constables handcuff both ladies and read them their rights.)

(The CHIEF walks away.)

ANTIGONE: Chief. You look at me! Just you wait, your time will come. I know it. You bastard, you better watch your back because if I have to, I will kill you with my own two hands –

CHIEF: Did you hear that? And you people as my witnesses, was that not uttering a death threat?

CONSTABLE BOUCHER: Yes, Chief. I believe so, got us a radical here, eh?

CHIEF: Not a radical, just stupid.

CONSTABLE BOUCHER: We will take them in to the detachment and you can come in and make your statement at the office. *(Leading ANTIGONE and ISMENE away.)*

(CHORUS enters.)

CHORUS: Antigone, you have gone too far,
Now you pay the dues of your father and brother.
To take the life of another is not your law either.
Your own blindness will destroy you.
Face the consequences, Antigone:
Be ready with your own hands of duty and honour.
Remember, you choose your fate.

Act II – Scene I

(Setting: CHIEF'S office. CHIEF is sitting in his desk. HAEMON enters.)

HAEMON: Father, I have come to see you about Antigone.

CHIEF: What? You heard the verdict of your bride? Well, she's not your bride anymore. I assume you don't agree with my decision?

HAEMON: No I don't, that's why I'm here. Leave her alone....

CHIEF: A wretched and outspoken woman you don't need. Women cannot contend with men, you see, Haemon, my son. A very important lesson...you deserve more.

HAEMON: I understand, Father. You taught me the concept of wanting more. Nothing would change your narrow mind.

CHIEF: Haemon, you are not angry with me are you?

HAEMON: Father, I will not disobey you. But do not speak of her that way, as just a woman. My mother is a woman and she is your wife. In all fairness, Father, women are the backbone of our culture.

CHIEF: No. I am the backbone.

HAEMON: Oh, Father, if only you could see reality. You don't know how to live life. You don't know how to love...love me or mother the way you should. Money and material things are not love. . .we could care less.

CHIEF: Your mother loves the bottle more than me. So why should I love her. Love is empty.

HAEMON: And how do you know?

CHIEF: Enough! Nevertheless, you would not want to marry someone like Antigone. She is not worthy of you. Let her go now, she can find someone of her own company.

Believe me, your heart will heal. You don't love her, you think you love her. It's all in your head. Never be inferior to your heart. Besides, you are too young to know any better.

HAEMON: Yes, Father. You are the wise one. I would never want to go against your word. How foolish of me.

CHIEF: That is good to hear. Are you going into town tonight? Here's some money. *(Handing him money.)*

HAEMON: No, I don't want money, and I am not going anywhere. I will just stay around here.

CHIEF: Well, do you need anything?

HAEMON: Yes, I do, Father, one thing.

CHIEF: What is it my son?

HAEMON: Why do you despise Polynices? What did he do to make you banish him?

CHIEF: *(Clears his throat.)* Well, it's a very long story. And I will not dwell on it. Polynices betrayed me and, more importantly, the reserve. I almost lost power because of him. That is why he was BCR'd from here. He was not true to the people, he was a man who wore two faces. Only I knew the real Polynices. He was greedy and only wanted money. That is what I gave him to get out of here.

HAEMON: What do you mean, money? That can't be the whole story. What is it?

CHIEF: *(Takes a deep breath.)* Polynices came into my office one day threatening to expose how I was spending the band monies. I had a business that no one knew about. Not even your mother. It was my own business venture. Anyway, I borrowed money from the band. Polynices found out about it. I told him to be loyal to me and not to speak one word to anyone. At that time Polynices was having financial difficulties. The motor had blown on his car and he needed a new one. So I offered him ten thousand dollars to forget my business. I gave him five thousand dollars up-front and I told him I would give him the remainder of the money the following week if he promised to leave the reserve. So he left and went to the city. After he left, I found out he stole financial files relating to the band deficit. I was very angry, so I did not pay him the rest of the money. He kept phoning me and he threatened to go to the RCMP and tell them that I was stealing money. Not only that, he was going to go public and call a meeting at the reserve and tell the people of what was going on. It wasn't what it seemed like, he made it sound worse. I didn't want him back on the reserve, so I drew up a Band Council Resolution for him to never enter the premises of the reserve again.

HAEMON: On what grounds?

CHIEF: That he stole the ten thousand dollars.

HAEMON: I thought you only gave him five thousand?

CHIEF: I did, but I made it look like he stole ten.

HAEMON: And that was the basis of your deranged BCR? You did worse.

CHIEF: Haemon, sometimes one's prosperity leads to another's destruction. To make it worse, he went to the media. The stress was unbearable, reporters, TV crews were everywhere. Bad press I don't need. I had to maintain my composure as the Chief during the media crisis. Councillor told them that Polynices has been BCR'd for stealing, and this was nothing but sour grapes. That's all we told them.

HAEMON: You lied to everybody. Father, how could you take money that isn't yours? How much did you take? And what kind of business was it, anyway?

CHIEF: It was ahh, ahh – shit, I might as well tell you. It was a gambling operation disguised as a strip club. I was trying to make more money by inviting only executives, like myself, into the club and the gambling operation that was underground. But the business, it doesn't matter any more, it doesn't exist. Haemon, you have to understand, it was borrowing. It's done all the time. I borrowed two hundred and fifty thousand dollars, and I intend to pay it all back.

HAEMON: Yeah, right, Father. How? Money from the band is what we survive on. What about mom, how could you have such a business? Don't you respect her just a little bit?

CHIEF: Your mother is just another drunk. She wouldn't have cared. I am not worried. You shouldn't worry, I will pay the money back.

HAEMON: I don't believe you. You say that Antigone and her family are corrupt, look at yourself. They are your scape-goat. I defend you, Father, against everyone when I should be kicking your ass. Look at you, no wonder we're screwed up. My mother is an alcoholic and you treat her like shit. Me, I can't even get my ass off the reserve. You taught me well. This place is nothing but a hellhole that makes people dependent. Dependent on government handouts. You sure are their friends down in Ottawa, saying nothing to advocate for your people. But you sure do a good job of taking money for yourself from them.

CHIEF: Haemon! That is enough!

HAEMON: You are the one that drives my mother to drinking, and today I wish I was never your son! You shouldn't have even adopted me! I hear you tell Mom that she is useless because she could not ever give you one biological child...

CHIEF: Haemon that is enough! You are my son, adopted or not! Your mother could never have children and she can't deal with it, so she drinks. Say no more, Haemon!

HAEMON: No, Father. I am tired of taking your shit. I will no longer defend you. Antigone is innocent of your empty accusations. Father, at least let her be free. Anger towards Antigone will not quench your rage towards Polynices. Ismene has nothing to do with these drummed up charges. I feel so much shame and sorrow in my heart to see others treated unjustly because of my father's greed. I want to be free from all of this...*(Haemon walks out.)*

CHIEF: *(Yells.)* Haemon! Haemon! Come back here. I will, I will let Ismene free. Do you hear me? Haemon...

Scene II

(Setting: RCMP detachment.)

ANTIGONE: *(Speaking to herself.)* Oh Great Spirit, look at me now. Here I stand alone, one person who stood up for what I believe in and now I'm condemned by my people. What are they afraid of? My people will lose all that they have if they don't stand up to their enemies. They will have to see that all the honour is in our roots and in the ancestral laws. Never the laws of man. Material things will get them nowhere. Where in heaven does money matter? Polynices, I have laid you to rest. My duty is done, and now I face my reward, the reward of defying his laws and taking into my own hands what I thought was fair. Therefore, I have honoured the laws that say you must be buried within four days. Now your spirit can join our ancestors in the spirit world. *kîwê* go home.

(HAEMON enters the detachment.)

CONSTABLE BOUCHER: What brings you here this time of night, Haemon?

Haemon: You have to help me please.

Constable Boucher: Is your father here to make his statement?

Haemon: Don't let my father know that I am here. Antigone and Ismene still here?

Constable Boucher: Ismene has been let go, we had no grounds to keep her. Antigone is still being held until the charges go through. I assume your father will be coming in to make his statement soon...

Haemon: I don't know his business. I need to see Antigone before she leaves. I know my father is getting rid of her. Can I see her? Please, I will do anything.

Constable Boucher: Hmmm. I don't know. I don't think your father would be too happy about that. *(Pauses.)* What the hell, go ahead. Only for awhile now.

(Leads Haemon to her cell.)

Haemon: Sure, I won't be long.

(Lets him into cell.)

Antigone: Haemon. *(She hugs him.)* What are you doing here? You should go, go now before your father finds out.

Haemon: No, Antigone. I came to see you before you leave. I wish that we could be together. I am weak Antigone, please forgive me. I am like any other person on the rez, I just can't leave. One way or another, I will find a way out just to see you. Maybe someday we will be together.

Antigone: Yes, maybe someday, Haemon. The bond we have will never be taken from us, ever. For now I understand that you do what you have to do, my love. I will not be angry.

HAEMON: *(Hugs ANTIGONE.)* Oh Antigone, I love you so much. *(Pauses.)* Remember the first time we danced?

ANTIGONE: Yes, I do. At the sports day dance. You didn't even ask me, you just pointed your lips towards the dance floor. And I went for it. How foolish.

HAEMON: I didn't have to say one word to get you to dance with me. Let's remember the good memories we had together. Antigone, let's dance.

(ANTIGONE points her lips to a clear space in the cell. They both giggle. ANTIGONE starts humming a familiar tune and they both dance.)

HAEMON: *(Stops and looks at ANTIGONE.)* I must leave now...

(CHIEF enters and interrupts.)

CHIEF: *(Outraged.)* Haemon! What are you doing here? How could you come and see her after I forbade you having anything to do with her?

HAEMON: Father, what makes you think that I would listen to you? You cannot break the bond we have, ever. Even when she is gone I will still love her, and there is nothing you can do to stop it.

CHIEF: Stop it! Quit speaking of love, you don't even know what love is. You are just a fool.

HAEMON: It takes a fool to know a fool, Father. You don't know what love is, you can't even be a husband or a father.

CHIEF: Constable, have Antigone transported off reserve land immediately. Even if you dump her off in the middle of nowhere.

(CONSTABLE BOUCHER puts ANTIGONE in handcuffs.)

(CHORUS enters as lights fade away.)

CHORUS:

Sadly dears, they are gone,
Soon their fates will come.
Antigone, you are wrong,
As a life is not taken, powerless, alone.
Be wary of your words,
The heavens above frown upon
The knives in the back, hateful words.
Time is near when all is gone.

Scene III

(Setting: CHIEF's office. The CHIEF is sitting in his office alone. The phone rings.)

CHIEF: Hello. Yes, that's good. Where did you drop her off? Oh I see, just as long as she is not on the reserve. Good for her, she needs to walk. Maybe she won't make it far, lots of drunks on the road tonight. Thank you for calling, Boucher. *(Pauses.)* Yeah, I will in the morning. How much do you want?

(TIRESIAS enters.)

CHIEF: All right, I said I'll pay you tomorrow, tax free...I got to go, I have a visitor. *(Hangs up phone.)* Tiresias, what favour brings you here on this stormy night?

TIRESIAS: None. Chief, though I cannot see all that is happening, I have come to warn you of bad things to come. *kiskêyihta kahkiyaw ôma kâ-tôtaman ohcitaw ka-tipahikân. cîki ôma êwako kîsikâw.* Understand that all you do you will pay for someday. That day is near. I come here as your friend and I have heard all that you have done. I feel sorry for you, Chief. It's my duty to bring warning.

CHIEF: Tiresias, I have never waived your advice before. Tell me, what could happen? I will listen to your wisdom and take into my hands what I have to do. I am curious what the future holds. You speak of bad things coming. What do you mean by that? Everybody and everything is on my side, you said!

TIRESIAS: Chief Creon, you are on the edge of fate, and you must come back to the reality that all is not based on your laws. There is something much more divine that ultimately rules these lands. Mediocrity is not distinguished, and the pride of one should never rule the hearts of many. It poisons the mind, you see. I am not here to condemn you, only to give warning. Chief, you cannot make people obey you and take into your hands any type of punishment. That is not your place. You are here to serve your people, they are not here to serve you. Look at yourself and try to see the wrongfulness of your pride. It's a crime in itself. Our people suffer your injustices; consequently you will encounter the most. I assure you that much. Chief, remember the storm you were so afraid of? That was a pure, innocent warning of hard times to come. You see, when man sows injustice on the earth, the spirits revolt through nature. When one creates injustice, everyone and everything will feel it, not only the person or persons that it is directed at. *kîkway kâ-mâyi-tôtaman, ôtê nîkân ka-pakamiskâkon, mâka ayiwâk ka-tôtâkon.* Everything travels in a cycle. What goes around, comes around, and when it comes back it is usually worse.

CHIEF: What are you saying I should do? Is it Antigone?

TIRESIAS: Yes, part of it. And part Polynices. Then the rest of your family and your people. Do something positive and bring Antigone back. Forgive her.

CHIEF: She threatened to kill me.

TIRESIAS: Yes, you brought that upon yourself. She is not your scapegoat. She is part of your people and your family. She belongs here. Remember that you are human and that we all make mistakes. As for Polynices, never kill the dead twice over. *okimâhkân, kâya kihcêyimiso, mâka manâtisi!* Swallow your pride, Chief, and be humble.

CHIEF: And how do you know that all your prophesizing isn't bullshit?

TIRESIAS: Truth is the greatest part of wisdom. I must leave now. Believe what you want to believe. *êkosi!*

(TIRESIAS exits and CHIEF is alone.)

CHIEF: Oh how could this be!
My own ugliness.
I am eaten by greed that my people never taught.
I have mastered it well.
I have learned resentment, power, and greed,
I have made my own brother
Jealous of my blood.
I see it now!
Help me please!
If it is not too late!

Scene IV

(Setting: CHIEF's office. COUNCILLOR enters)

COUNCILLOR: Tiresias just left. Chief, Tiresias sees people for one reason. If it's any consolation, Chief, Tiresias is never wrong. She only speaks the truth. You should take her advice.

CHIEF: There is truth in her words. Do you think I can redeem myself, Councillor?

COUNCILLOR: I don't know.

CHIEF: I must go find Antigone. Bring her back.

Scene V

(Setting: CHIEF's office. COUNCILLOR is looking out the window, it is storming. CONSTABLE BOUCHER enters.)

CONSTABLE BOUCHER: Councillor, where is the Chief?

COUNCILLOR: He has gone to find Antigone.

CONSTABLE BOUCHER: I have some news. It's not good. *(Pauses.)* We just found Haemon off the reserve by the creek. The car is unrecognizable, Antigone was with him. They are both dead.

(EURYDICE enters)

EURYDICE: Where's my husband, that bloody no good for nothing bastard? Did my ears hear you right? You are not speaking of Haemon?

CONSTABLE BOUCHER: I'm sorry...

EURYDICE: You're not sorry. My only son, my only child. It's all Creon's fault. He should have let them be.

(CONSTABLE BOUCHER leaves. COUNCILLOR hugs EURYDICE.)

EURYDICE: Where is he? The almighty Chief? My husband?

COUNCILLOR: He went to find Antigone.

EURYDICE: A little late for that. I am leaving to see my son one last time. My beloved son...I will be with him. *(She leaves.)*

COUNCILLOR: No! You can't drive. You're drunk. *(Speaking to himself.)*

(CHIEF enters.)

CHIEF: I could not find her. I don't know what to do.

COUNCILLOR: Chief, it's too late.

CHIEF: What do you mean?

COUNCILLOR: Antigone has died – and so has – Haemon!

CHIEF: Are you sure? Not Haemon.

COUNCILLOR: Boucher was here to give you the news when you were gone. Eurydice was here too. She went to the scene of the accident.

CHIEF: I must go there at once. Where are they?

Scene VI

(Setting: Scene of accident.)

PANOON: Eurydice came to the scene. She came to say goodbye to Haemon and Antigone and held a rifle under her chin and shot herself through the head. I'm sorry, Chief.

CHIEF: NO! Not my family! Please no! This is not real. This just can't be happening. Why are you telling me this? I can feel the pain, it breaks my heart. My family is gone, my fate has caught up to me. They are all gone. Look at me now. I no longer exist. For I am burdened with my own curse. I face the justice set before me in pure truth. I am the murderer. Take me away. I am too cowardly to take my own life. Help me, somebody help me. I am the fool of all fools. My fate falls on me now like the storm who falls on mother earth. *(Clenching his fists.)* Look at me! Down on my knees, brought to the realm of common ground. Without my family, my people, I am nothing! Nothing! Take pity on me! *(Falls to the ground.)*

Scene VII

Chorus:

Ah! We see the destruction of one
Becomes the destruction of all.
The laws of *kisê-manitow*
Are the laws for all creation:
To live in equality and harmony.
The blows of fate mercilessly teach wisdom.

(Chorus fades)

Guide to the Pronunciation of Cree Dialogue in

Antigone

Jean L. Okimâsis and Arok Wolvengrey

In the following list of the Cree vocabulary found in *Antigone,* an approximate English pronunciation is given for each word, phrase, or sentence, along with a translation. The pronunciation is broken into syllables with primary stress indicated in FULL CAPS, while secondary stress is given in SMALL CAPS. An example of this is as follows:

maskisin . . . . *"shoe, moccasin"*
[MUSS kis SIN]

The Cree word *maskisin,* "shoe, moccasin," thus follows the same stress pattern as the English word "medicine," with primary stress on the first syllable, and a small amount of secondary stress on the final syllable.

Act I – Scene I

p. 101. **tânisi!** . . . . *"hello"*
[TAAN sih]
cwâ! . . . . *"expression of disgust"*
[CHAW]

p. 105. **cwâ!** . . . . *"expression of disgust"*
[CHAW]
êkosi . . . . *"So, that's it!"*
[AY koo SIH]

p. 106. **hay hay!** . . . . *"Thank you!"*
[high HIGH]

p. 109. **kîminîcâkanak** . . . . *"bastards"*
[KEE min nee TSAA gun NUCK]

p. 122. **kîwê** . . . . *"go home"*
[kee WAY]

p. 125. **kiskêyihta kahkiyaw** . . . . *"understand (that) all ..."*
[kiss KAY yih tuh KUHK kee YOW]
ôma kâ-tôtaman . . . . *"... that you do ..."*
[oh MUH kaa TOTE tuh MUN]
ohcitaw ka-tipahikân. . . . . *"... you must pay for."*
[OH tsih TAO kuh tip PUH hig GAAN]
cîki ôma êwako kîsikâw. . . . . *"That day is near."*
[tsee KIH oh MAY wuck co KEE sick COW]

p. 126. **kîkway kâ-mâyi-tôtaman,** . . . . *"That which you do ..."*
[kee GWHY kaa MY yih TOTE tu MUN]
ôtê nîkân ka-pakamiskâkon,
. . . . *"... it will strike you in the future, ..."*
[oh TAY nee GAAN kuh PUCK kum MISS kaa KOON]
mâka ayiwâk ka-tôtâkon. . . . . *"... but even moreso."*
[maa GUY yuh WAAK kuh TOTE taa KOON]

p. 127. **okimâhkân,** . . . . *"Chief, ..."*
[oh KIM maah KAAN]
kâya kihcêyimiso, ... *"don't be (over) proud ..."*
[kie YUH KEEHT tsay YIM miss SO]
mâka manâtisi! . . . . *"but be respectful!"*
[maa GUH mun NAA tiss SIH]

p. 127. **êkosi** . . . . *"So, that's it!"*
[AY koo SIH]

p. 130. **kisê-manitow,** . . . . *"the Creator"*
[KISS say MUN toe]

Acknowledgements

My influence in writing plays came from director and playwright Floyd Favel, who encouraged me to write my adaptation of *Antigone.* Under Floyd's direction I read Sophocle's original play and soon came to see how the themes and issues in it are relevant to what is happening on First Nation reserves in Saskatchewan today.

This adaptation is set on a contemporary Indian reserve. To properly understand the plot, one must understand its context. In late 19TH century, Indian people agreed to share their land with the arriving European settlers. These arrangements were formalized and legalized through treaty. More than a century of colonial policies has led to the situation portrayed in this play.

Antigone was presented as a staged reading by the Red Tattoo Ensemble of Regina, in October 1988, at The Globe Theatre, Sandbox Series. It premiered as a workshop production in Regina, in 2001, by Curtain Razors and the Red Tattoo Ensemble. The cast included Monique Mojica, Floyd Favel, Fawn Redwood, Ryan Atimoyoo, Maureen Belanger, Michele Sereda, Val Kinistino, and Preston LeCaine.

My thanks to Floyd Favel, and Michele Sereda for working with me in getting *Antigone* to the stage.

Bruce E. Sinclair

I would like to dedicate this play to my mother, Doreen Sinclair, my wife, Lucie Joyal, and my son, David Jacob Martin. I love you all. Thank you for everything precious you have given me.

characters (in order of appearance)

MARY OF PATUANAK – *Dene, thirties*

DENE MAN – *trapper, medicine man, fifties*

MAHKÊSÎS – *Cree, radio personality, forties*

JOE – *carpenter, Métis – Cree, thirties*

FREDDIE – *labourer, Métis, early twenties*

MAGGIE – *elder, Saulteaux, fifties*

GEORGE – *professor, Native Studies, white, fifties*

WILLOW – *professor, Native Studies, Mohawk, twenties*

KENNY – *professor, Native Studies, Shuswap, twenties*

DREAM SPIRITS – *entire cast, except for MARY*

Note: MAHKÊSÎS and DENE MAN can be played by one actor. As well, FREDDIE and KENNY can be played by one actor.

production notes

As *Mary of Patuanak* has yet to be produced, essential staging, artistic creation, and freedom can be explored. It is important to create suspension with Mary's bed as well as a place for the Dene Man and Mahkêsîs to appear and reappear within the darkness of the above world.

Trimester One

Scene I – Mary

(Lights come up on a single bed that is suspended in the air on the stage with a figure wrapped in a colourful quilt of a patchwork design of stars and geometric shapes. The bed is old-fashioned and painted beige. Suspended by the bed is a crucifix with plastic flowers attached. A poster of Buffy Sainte-Marie adorns the wall. A wooden table with radio and mismatched chairs are beside the bed. A black and white photo of a woman kneeling beside a moose is in a wooden frame on the table. A pile of thick books and a knapsack hanging from one of the chairs complete the picture. Gradually the lights shift to a dim aura as a drumbeat softly announces the change in mood. A chant emerges from the drum, fading and echoing, with the volume slowly increasing as the lights create an image of dreamy suspension. A figure is lit, resembling a human being suspended on a cross from a rosary. The figure slowly lowers toward the sleeping MARY *and a barely audible voice begins a gentle Dene chant. Finally,* MARY *stirs and moans and pushes the covers back. She begins to awaken, sensing something in the room with her. She sees the figure hovering near the foot of her bed.)*

DENE MAN: *Kozigal…kozigal….s'ekwi……….s'ekwi……..*
sèkwi degai hi nigha ha

*(*MARY *closes her eyes and repeats the words, stumbling over them like a child. The figure seems to acknowledge the attempt to speak and begins to move away as the lights and drum/chant reverberate and fade, leaving only the sound of Mary's voice whispering the words. She sits in the bed, transfixed. Lights fade.)*

Scene II – MAHKESIS's Tune

(Sun comes up brightly on MARY*. The radio alarm kicks in.)*

MAHKÊSÎS: *(Disembodied voice.)* Well….Well….Welll….gooooood morning to all you boys and girls, *awâsisak*…wake up...get the hell outa bed...the sun is waiting to greet you again. Dream time is over, children...the full circle of the sun is here again, just as it always has been... for all you people that have to go work.... Tooooo bad...it's seven in the a.m.... Remember how it used to be before somebody plugged into that concept of time... to regulate you...to control you...long ago...*kayâsi-nêhiyaw...* Our people knew where the sun was in the sky and what it meant.... They knew which way the wind blew and where it came from.... They looked at time through the eyes of the animals and the birds and the sky and learned how to live and survive. It's so different now, wouldn't you say? Dead skunks everywhere. Ain't it the truth? It really is time to wake up, folks, and remember. Oh, I know... ol' Mahkêsîs is just being mean this morning. After all it is Monday, *tâpwê...* forgive me.... Well, don't you worry your little head about it. I got just what you're looking for...a little song by those boys from Sandy Bay, Saskatchewan, Youngblood...and "Growing Up In the Wild".... Just remember where you heard it, folks...right here on CHIP 90.5 FM.... Red Skies.... The voice of the people, naturally right here in Saskabush...your voice...and don't forget it! Aaaahhh!

(Song begins. MARY begins to dress. Lights down.)

Scene III – Street

(In the dark we hear the sound of the city. This city is Saskatoon, Saskatchewan. Lights up on MARY pushing a shopping cart down the street. The cart has a hawk feather attached to it and is filled with odds and ends, bottles, cans, a discarded toy and a toy doll. MARY is dressed in jeans and a jean jacket, a little sloppy but clean. She is reading her notebook.)

MARY: ...How can I tell you of my love... strong as an eagle... soft as a dove... and as patient as a pine tree which stands in the sun... *

* This poem was written by an anonymous student at Joe Duquette High School in Saskatoon, circa 1991.

(We hear a voice from a vehicle yell.)

VOICE: Hey! Get off the street and get a job, you stupid squaw!

(Laughter, tires squeal, car fades into the distance.)

MARY: Aw shuttup.........honky cat! *(Pause.)* ....which whispers in the wind you are the one... *(Stops.)* Not too bad, sister,...not bad at all...aaah...I'm just proud now.

(Lights up on garbage collection, boxes, etc. MARY parks her cart, starts rummaging. JOE appears, haggard, carrying garbage bag.)

JOE: Hey.

MARY: *(Startled.)* Oh shit....sorry.

JOE: Are you hungry ?

MARY: No no...not that bad. I'm just looking for some stuff.

JOE: I thought it was cats out here.

MARY: Meoooowww...no it's just me.

JOE: If you don't mind me asking, what are you looking for?

MARY: Can you keep a secret?

JOE: Huh?

MARY: I'm looking for lost dreams.

JOE: Oh....OK. *(Laughs.)* So... *(Points to cart.)* Is that yours?

MARY: I'm just minding my own business, OK? *(Turns to leave.)*

JOE: Wait....really...what are you looking for?

MARY: I told you already....do you have a problem?

JOE: I don't know.... I...haven't lost any dreams lately...I think.... Hey! How would you know if you lost a dream anyways?

MARY: You'd just know it.

JOE: Who are you?

MARY: An Indian....just like you. My name is Mary.

JOE: *(Extends hand.)* Joe...your next nightmare *(No reaction.)* ...well...I better get going....

(MARY begins to get morning sickness.)

JOE: What's the matter?

(MARY sinks to her knees. JOE attempts to help her. MARY gets sick on JOE)

JOE: Oh, shit. Damnit. Are you OK?

MARY: Oh...oh...I'm sorry...I gotta go...find a bathroom. *(Exits without cart.)*

JOE: *(Yelling.)* Are you gonna make it? Mary?...Mary?

(Lights down. James Brown's "I Feel Good" jumps to the beat.)

Scene IV – MAGGIE

(Lights come up on MAGGIE's kitchen. James Brown continues to cook loud. MAGGIE is kneading bannock on a table to the beat and singing along, gyrating her hips. A braid of sweetgrass is suspended in the air. Hank Williams Sr. captured in B & W is framed on the wall. Muskeg tea is boiling happily away on a white chipped stove. She's wearing a jean jacket with a flower printed dress complete with bare feet. She is timeless. Across the stage a spot picks up MARY walking slowly toward MAGGIE's house. She stops just before the "entrance.")

MARY: Buffalo spirit...hear me.... Long ago I waited for the sound of your thunder, the dust from your hooves. We prayed for you to come and now we celebrate your return. Our children scream with laughter when they see us riding in the mist dragging you in the travois...And when the red sun sinks silently in the West, we know that we will eat and dance with the juice running down from our mouths.

(Lights return to MAGGIE groovin'. Song ends.)

MAHKÊSÎS: *(As MAHKÊSÎS' voice breaks through the airwaves, we discern his presence suspended stage left. Lighting is such that we only see a black figure lit by incredible luminous dials. He will never be completely visible throughout the play.)* I'm back and I'm black...just kidding James Brown... Hey...you know, a long time ago when the U.S. Cavalry used to chase down our brothers down South, the Sioux, Cheyenne, Comanche and Apache, they had some black brothers who fought with the white soldiers. When our people saw the black man for the first time, he called them buffalo soldiers because of those tight curls.... No kidding.... Up here us Cree called them *kaskitêwiyâs*.... Bob Marley wrote a song about it called "Buffalo Soldier," and that's what we're going to play for you lucky boys and girls out there in radioland.... So remember our black brothers as we honour their music and try to communicate...everything, everything gonna be alright...here on Red Skies 90.5 FM...the rhythm of the nation.

(MARY knocks on the door. It opens. MAGGIE turns down music and turns, sees MARY.)

MAGGIE: Whoooahh! Where'd you come from?

MARY: Sorry..the door opened.... The music was kinda loud.... I'm Mary...the one that phoned.

MAGGIE: I remember...*âstam*....come in.

(MARY enters, stands awkwardly.)

Mary: That Mahkêsîs is pretty crazy, huh? I wake up to his voice every morning.

Maggie: Too bad it's not the real thing, eh?

Mary: What?

Maggie: You know he says that FM stands for funny man.

Mary: Funny man? So what does AM stand for?

Maggie: Angry man?

Mary: Oh.

Maggie: Anyways, come in...I got some muskeg tea going to beat sixty. Sit down girl, take it easy.

(Mary sits.)

Maggie: So...it's Mary, isn't it?

Mary: I got your number from my prof, Willow Carter. I wasn't sure how to make an appointment with an elder. Oh yeah...I almost forgot *(Giggles.)* Here. *(Tosses pack of tobacco to Maggie who, surprised, catches it. Long pause.)* Did I do something wrong?

Maggie: My girl, you shouldn't throw tobacco at an elder...this is a sacred thing to be treated with respect.

Mary: OOOps! Sorry...I guess I've got lots to learn.

Maggie: *(Laughs.)* That's OK. Next time you'll know. So you're Chipewyan?

Mary: How'd you know that?

Maggie: The way you threw the tobacco at me. *(Pause.)* Just kidding.

MARY: You're a funny woman. I'm from Patuanak...at least I was a long time ago. I'm not so sure anymore. I just don't feel a connection to that place.

MAGGIE: When's the last time you went home?

MARY: That's just it. I can't remember ever being there.

MAGGIE: There's some nice people there. Let me think. I just can't remember their last names. I have it written down.

MARY: I don't know anybody from there...I was adopted when I was little and I'm just trying to find out...don't know where to start.

MAGGIE: There's a lot about the past that's hard to understand. Some say it's better to leave it alone...some have to know everything. You don't have to feel like you have to tell me everything.

MARY: What makes you think I'll tell you everything? *(Long pause.)* Oh shit. Sorry. I mean it's not really my parents I'm wondering about. They're dead anyways...but my other relatives...the ones from the past...a long time ago...

(MARY stands and begins to sway as in a trance, MAGGIE stares, MARY laughs.)

MARY: I've been dreaming...lots and lots of dreams...scary...I'm scared...too many fucking dreams.

MAGGIE: Mary, I'm right here beside you...take my hand.

(MARY takes her hand, and then begins to sob. MAGGIE hugs and holds her.)

MARY: These dreams, Maggie...they're so strong...they scare the shit outa me...sometimes...but sometimes I wake up and it's good. I feel warm and like...my family is with me.... *(Stop.)* Do you think I'm retarded or what?

MAGGIE: It's OK, Mary. Do you want to lie down?

MARY: No....thanks. Most of the time they talk to me in this language...I think it's Dene...you know, Chipewyan.... This man and woman and two kids.... All of them take turns talking to me like I'm right there in their home. It's so real....*`sekwi degai hi nigha ha.*

MAGGIE: Mary, you're standing on my foot.

MARY: Oh sorry.... Sometimes I'm in a rocking chair.... Sometimes they talk to me like I'm a baby... y'know... making little noises and faces and teaching me little words like parents do....And it's a long time ago...the house is in the bush, a lean-to or something like that.... They're dressed in furs and deerskins...winter, and the fire is always going...I hear dogs yelping...they treat me so good...they look at me like they love me.

(MARY sits in the chair. MAGGIE rubs her foot.)

MAGGIE: That must make you feel pretty good.

MARY: It does. Do you know what it means?

MAGGIE: No, Mary. I don't...and I have another appointment.

(They both laugh.)

MARY: You're the first person I ever told this to.... I had to tell somebody.

MAGGIE: And you had to pick me? Just jokes, Mary...what about your friends?

MARY: No...nobody.

MAGGIE: We're alone here.

MARY: I just asked Willow if there was somebody that might know...

MAGGIE: I don't know what they mean, I drink tea, I don't read them, but we can talk though..maybe we can work something out. At least we'll eat some bannock, huh? You should go back to Patuanak. The dreams are in your language. You don't speak it?

MARY: I'm trying to learn though.... I found this old Dene dictionary...found this word. It's really beautiful...it means Moonbeam...but I'm having a helluva time learning. Its hard...really hard...you always have to have spit in your mouth.

MAGGIE: It's good you're trying to learn.

MARY: I think I've learned some words from the dreams. *Ene...seta....* I wake up saying them...words for mother and father...I'm sure that's what they mean.

MAGGIE: I heard there's a ceremony taking place in Patuanak this winter...an old ceremony...maybe this is a good time for you to go home...and those dreams...you have a power, Mary. I think your relatives passed on something to you...a gift.

MARY: A gift?

MAGGIE: You look tired girl..I'll get you some tea...lie down on the couch for awhile.

MARY: Do you have cable? *(Laughs.)* There's just one more thing. Last night I thought I saw Jesus on the cross...only he had moccasins on...whaddya think?

MAGGIE: I wish I could dream like you. *(Turns on the radio.)* Here, maybe Mahkêsîs will make you feel at home too.

MARY: *(Lies on couch, closes eyes.)* I am tired. Maybe you're right...go back to Patuanak.

(Lights fade on MARY and MAGGIE.)

MARY: *(In darkness.)* Buffalo spirit...you are one of us just as we are one of you...come join us in our lodges and share our pipe and our songs and our stories. It will be a good day for both of us.

(Lights come up on MAHKÊSÎS hunched over controls. Silhouette spot on MARY sleeping and MAGGIE smudging.)

MAHKÊSÎS: *wâcistakâc*...yesssirreeee...tonight's turning out to be a beautiful night. Spring here in Toon town and life is pretty damn good...sooooo goood. For all you listeners out there I want you to think about just that...how life is so good to us human beings, the two legged ones, and all the things in the world we have. Remember where we came from. Remember your mom and dad, our grandparents, *kôkom* and *mošôm*, our elders. Go out there and find them, visit them. Cook them something. Take them to...the bingo.... Aaaaahhhhhh. Just kidding, but do something, anything, everything. It's time for some more good music...here's a new one by Chester Knight and the Wind and a little ditty called "Love Me Strong." This is the night calling CHIP 90.5 FM Red Skies...a time of change, a time to celebrate...

(Lights down.)

Scene V – The Wise Ones

(Lights up on a room with degrees suspended in the air in profusion. An elderly, sophisticated white man in his fifties stands centre stage dominating the room. He is dressed in a conservative grey tweed suit garnished with an expensive Italian shirt. He is holding a glass of red wine. Across from him upstage is an Indian woman also holding a glass of wine. Arms folded, musing over something amusing. She is in her late twenties, bold, confident, wearing jeans and a casual top with a silver bracelet. Behind her, sitting in a loveseat, is an Indian man in a Cowichan sweater clutching a Corona beer. Downstage left, a spot comes up on MAGGIE laboriously fleshing a moosehide throughout the entire following dialogue.)

George: I agree with you, Miss Carter, women in the fur trade were definitely a factor in the creation of economic prosperity for the company.

Willow: ...but were treated like shit ...or excrement to you, sir..regardless.

George: *(Chuckles.)* Yes...that is a term that would apply.... Recognition for women was virtually non-existent and....

Willow: Not then and not now...Professor.

Maggie: Pick up a bone scraper and tell me about it.

George: Equality can be somewhat elusive at times...yes... however we should get to the business at hand... Willow...Kenny...you have both worked very hard to get to this position, and I must tell you I'm honoured to be working with both of you.

Kenny: Likewise...George.

George: I've been going over your theses and, as you are both aware, the department agrees in principle with your ideas, and the project has been approved.... All we have to do now is figure out how the hell we're going to accomplish our collective vision.... Where do we begin?

Kenny: Simplistically put, sir, a hands-on approach, going into the communities to collect the data ourselves...meet with the elders...bring in the subjective equation.

Maggie: Ooooh those five dollar words make me crazy, honey.

Willow: ...the subjective equation...you mean...actually talking to people.

George: It's rough to talk to the elders in the North...I can't speak Cree or Dene...and I don't know if they even want to speak to us.

Maggie: Get to work. Did you forget how to work?

Willow: Actually, George, we're in the same boat in some respects.... We're not Cree or Dene either.

Maggie: *kikiyâskin.* I know a few words I can teach you.

Kenny: I have a suggestion. The Meadow Lake Tribal Council has an economic strategy in place that could translate into billions...booming forestry industry, hydroelectric dams and uranium in the North...I'm telling you...it's...

Willow: There's a lot more to it than that, Kenny. The North is a dynamic, thriving culture that is threatened by these megaprojects.... A lot of the people are on welfare, unemployed. What you're talking about is an elite group investing in themselves.... These people need more than promises of work.

Maggie: They couldn't even make a fire if they had a match.

Kenny: You don't know that!

Willow: You got to be kidding. I say we should concentrate on traditional values...the culture...the languages.

Kenny: The only tradition that matters now is cold, hard cash, baby. That's the name of the game. Economic security. The culture is a thing of the past.

Willow: Maybe for you..and I'm not your baby. For me, that bush represents a lot more than a billion telephone books in Tokyo. There's history there, stories, legends.

Maggie: If I knew how to write, I'd write you a cheque. But since I don't have any money, I'll tell you a story.

George: Well, well, the department really cooked up a mulligan stew with you two. However, I do have a proposal here that might interest you. The department has got wind of a unique development that's unfolding in the North....

Actually, Kenny...it's in the Meadow Lake Tribal Council... Patuanak to be exact. The word is that a ceremony or event is going to take place this winter that will impact upon the North. The problem is we don't know when or what is going to take place...all we know is where.

KENNY: Something's going on up there but we don't know what it is? I don't get it.

WILLOW: You think it might be a ceremony...a sacred ceremony of some kind?

GEORGE: Why is it such a secret?

WILLOW: If the Indians up there are preparing for a ceremony, why is the Native Studies Department so bent on knowing the details? Surely the ceremony is none of their business. Wait! There's a woman in my class...Mary...she's from Patuanak.... Unfortunately, she's not doing so good.

MAGGIE: I know a good prayer in Latin...but I forgot.

GEORGE: Oh?

WILLOW: I don't think she's university material...kind of a dreamer.

GEORGE: I wish I could afford to dream.

WILLOW: Me too.

KENNY: So what are we doing?

GEORGE: Let's explore this idea further.... This could be a secret ceremony that the department would love to know more about...and we all want to succeed in our academic pursuits, true?

KENNY: Cheers.

GEORGE: Apparently, the Dene are historic enemies of the Cree, and are still resistant to outsiders. So that might be a good thing, since you're not Cree. Out of curiosity, what tribe are you two from?

WILLOW: I'm Mohawk from Akwesasne.

KENNY: Land of butter and barricades *(Willow glares at him.)* I'm from BC.

WILLOW: Oh, the British Columbian tribe.

GEORGE: Do you two also have a history of aggression? *(Dead silence.)* Well...yes...maybe you were too tired to fight after climbing mountains, and you, Willow, were busy with massacre with the French, was it? More wine, me hearties?

KENNY: I'll stick to beer.

GEORGE: Willow?

WILLOW: Thanks. So...Professor...what tribe do you belong to?

GEORGE: The last of the pseudo-intellectual palefaces.... Polish sausage and Czech meatballs. Canadian.

WILLOW: That reminds me of a good joke.

GEORGE: Please enlighten me.

WILLOW: Ever since I was a little girl I've always longed secretly to be white.

GEORGE: Really? Okay, I'll bite. Why?

WILLOW: So I can be head of the Native Studies Department.

(Everybody, including MAGGIE, laughs except GEORGE who joins in momentarily.)

MAGGIE: Education is our buffalo.

(Lights down.)

Scene VI – Joe

(In the dark we hear the sound of a woodsaw. Lights up on the silhouette of a man with a hardhat with a feather inspecting a two-by-four. He is wearing a plaid shirt, jeans and workboots. He is clean-cut, Métis and in his thirties.)

JOE: Working in the old fort, workin' with the ol' farts, going down down...working in the gold mine, gold mine... whoops, gotta sit down...workin'...workin' in the ol' mine.

(FREDDIE, a young man, enters wearing another hardhat and a muscle shirt. He is Indian and in his twenties.)

FREDDIE: There he is working agin...c'mon Joe, knock it off. You're making the rest of us look bad.

JOE: What time is it anyways?...oh, ten after...the company gets some free labour, huh? I just want to finish this fucking order. Catch up with you boys.

FREDDIE: Forget it, Jack! Let's get the fuck outa here...long weekend man. You said you'd give me a ride home. C'mon man, it's party time!

JOE: So what are you punks doing this weekend?

FREDDIE: Party hardy, Joe. Drive up to Edmonchuck and check out some peelers. Wanna come?

JOE: Naw. No time for that shit. I'll probably just stick around.

FREDDIE: I don't know, Joe. You know what they say. All work and no play makes Joe a boring piece of shit.

JOE: Look...if you punks want to watch some strippers take it all off...blow your wad... *(Stops, remembers song, sings.)* ...Took my money like I knew they would, mama,...ooooh woooo, feeling fine, mama.... Do do da de dum.... Hey, you, remember that one?...great cut.

FREDDIE: A guy's gotta get laid sometime, Joe. If you don't use it, you'll lose it. Some of the boys are starting to talk.

JOE: Let 'em talk, let 'em talk.... The way you boys use it, it'll probably just fall off.

FREDDIE: C'mon, Joe, get a life.

JOE: You guys go ahead.... Get your kicks.... I'm just not into it.

FREDDIE: So what are you into?

JOE: Say.... Do you have a toke?

FREDDIE: Maybe.

JOE: Listen, you little fucker, do you want a ride home or not? And what about that fifty bucks you owe me, guy? Before you stick it in a G-string.

FREDDIE: Yeah, yeah. You'll get it. Don't sweat it.... I'm a little short this paycheque.

JOE: Sure, sure. Hey...by the way...have you seen that woman on 20th Street with that shopping cart....Indian...not bad looking?

FREDDIE: Woman? Yeah! I remember her. Strange days, Joe. For sure. *(Pause.)* No, ain't seen her. Why?

JOE: Huh?...oh nothing...just curious.

FREDDIE: I'm telling you, Joe. She's looney toons...for sure.... Time's awasting. Let's get outa this fucking place.

JOE: Yeah, let's go. *(They both exit.)*

Scene VII – School Days

(Lights come up on Mary *sitting in her chair writing feverishly. Around her are balls of crumpled up paper. Finally she finishes writing and stands with a sheaf of papers in her hand.)*

Mary: Yeah! Gotcha, Professor.

(Lights dim as Mary *stretches, turns the radio on)*

Mahkêsîs: Ah....*tânisi,* my friends,...welcome back to the sounds of your people...the first peoples...the First Nations.... It's getting late, kids...but I'll tell ya...what a day...a big day for us Aboriginal students...*nêhiyawak*...uh huh.... It's crunch time...final exams. White knuckle time at the University of Saskatchewan, come to think of it, it's white all over there in that ol' fort. You know, my children, much has changed since the great chiefs signed those treaties so long ago.... Who would have thought our people would be entering these institutions in such large numbers? Give up? The answer is...those very same grandfathers and grandmothers knew.... They knew that we would have to survive and we would have to adapt to those white ways. They could see what we had to give up...our land for their promises.... And did you know, my children, there are well over 400 of us here now? There is so much to learn and so much to share. Don't you forget...you have a lot to teach these people, as well. It's been a long time comin', oh yes it has.... Now *awâsisak... wakanyeja*...my children...this gift of education is for our future...our children...our sacred children. So take care of it...just as we are sacred. Listen to your heart...your spirit. Ho. Here is an offering now from one of our ol' buddies from the Piapot Reserve in the South.... You know who I'm talking about...eh?...Buffy Sainte-Marie and "We're Only Getting Started".... As for you students, we'll see you in four years or so with your degree and your eagle feather....

(Song begins. Mary *begins to prepare for bed. Lights dim.* Mary *walks slowly back to her bed and lies down. Lights dim. In the low light,*

MARY remembers something and sits up and sets the radio alarm. She then falls back and falls asleep. Lights change to dream sequence. A drumbeat emerges, but this time it is a live drum held by a figure emerging from the darkness. It is a man with a cap and checkered jacket common in the bush. He appears oblivious to MARY and is signing a chant with the drum. The drum and the chant become louder. Lights go black momentarily and then come up on the DENE MAN sitting in the chair watching MARY sleep. MARY begins to stir and then rolls over and sees the DENE MAN.)

MARY: AAAAHHH! What are you doing here? Who are you ? *(Jumps out of bed.)* Where are we ? Please....please. You're scaring me! Please tell me why you keep coming here! I don't understand.... Please leave me alone!

DENE MAN: *S'ekwi...sèkwi degai hi nigha ha...s'ekwi degai hi nigha ha.*

MARY: I'm trying to learn but it's hard. I can't think! I want to answer you but I...I....

DENE MAN: *(Holds out his hand.) kozigal...kozigal.......sèkwi degai hi nigha ha.*

(Lights fade, DENE MAN disappears, MARY stares. Lights down.)

Scene VIII – Connection

(Spotlight comes up on MAGGIE knocking softly on MARY's door. Another spot comes up on MARY sobbing in her bed. MARY stops sniffling, goes to door, stands there. MAGGIE knocks again.)

MARY: Who is it ?

MAGGIE: Mary? Is that you? It's Maggie.

MARY: *(Opens door a crack.)* I'm sorry, Maggie, I'm just not feeling very good right now.

MAGGIE: I thought there was something wrong. I've got some good news for you.

MARY: What?

MAGGIE: Do you remember when you were talking about your dreams and the people talking to you in Dene?

MARY: Yes.

MAGGIE: Well, I remembered my friend up there in Patuanak, so I thought I'd try and find him. So I looked him up in the phone book. Well, actually, there was about six of them...I called anyways, and the first one was his niece, who gave me his number. So I called and there he was after all these years. I told him about you and your dreams and he said he'd like to meet you. He knows everything about that area. He's an elder now.

MARY: Maybe I should just leave these things alone.

MAGGIE: Sure Mary. You call me anytime. You don't sound very good. Are you sick?

MARY: I just need some sleep, OK?

MAGGIE: I told him those words you were trying to find out about...remember? And he said, like a child and a gift of some kind...my Dene is rusty. Does that help at all?

MARY: *(Momentarily shocked.)* I need some time to think. Everthing is happening too fast.

MAGGIE: Mary, you're not alone in this world. You have many friends and relatives that you don't know. You're going to be a mother soon. You have to get ready for the baby. Rest and pray, my girl. I'll light some sweetgrass for you. *(Silence.)* Good night child.

(MAGGIE exits. MARY goes to her bed, lies down. Lights dim. Clock radio breaks in.)

MAHKÊSÎS: Guess what? It's time to get up and go take care of that fire, my people. You got it right. Another day is here and it's time to rise and greet it in a good way. They say this is the coldest time of the night, just before the sun comes up so make sure your tipi is nice and warm when your children open their little eyes. Speaking of children, I've been learning about some of the Cree customs when a baby is born.... What they would do was take the after-birth, the placenta, and wrap it in a hide and put it in the trees for the spirits to look after...and when they cut the cord, they would keep it and put it in an ornamental bag for the child to wear around his neck. Amazing, huh? We have forgotten so much, my children.... A different way of life...and you know, it wasn't that long ago. Different nations have different customs. Here in Saskatchewan, we have six Nations...let's count them.... We have the Cree, Saulteaux, Dene, Dakota, Assiniboine, and our halfbreed brothers, the Métis. All right here in Saskatchewan, the land of the fast flowing river. Let's show our appreciation to all these nations whenever we can.... After all we are all one people...eeeyeeee.... Damn I'm profound this morning....whadddya say? You want some music? Coming right up. We just happen to have a beautiful morning song by that Métis songbird from Ile-la-Crosse, Cheryl Ogram, so don't you dare go back to sleep...oh no no no...get up and make yourself useful. Here comes Cheryl, right here on Red Skies.

(Sun lightens the room as song plays. Lights dim on bedroom and come up on WILLOW's classroom.)

Scene IX – Education

(Lights up again in MARY's bedroom. She is feverishly putting some notes and books into her knapsack, cursing to herself. Lights come up on WILLOW, also listening to the radio, glancing at her notes, she turns off the radio, stands, smiles at the class.)

WILLOW: As you can see, ladies and gentlemen, Indian women have been mistreated, abused and generally enslaved by our patriarchal society before, during, and after first contact. I give you these facts not as a vindictive feminist, but as a teacher imploring you to examine your own role, your own history and your own position regarding these painful and urgent issues. There is a lot of work to be done...so many wounds to heal and so much to look to in the future. Unfortunately, we are pressed for time...as it is this class which is now history. We will see you Thursday at the Arts building.... Have a nice day.

(As WILLOW *turns to examine some notes,* MARY *enters, dishevelled, obviously panic stricken.)*

MARY: Willow, could I have a word with you?

WILLOW: Mary, I'm sorry...I told you how I feel about you coming late to my lectures. This is ridiculous. The class is over and you show up here...

MARY: Look, I'm sorry. I couldn't get to sleep last night and I had this dream...

WILLOW: Mary, how many times in the past month have you given me a story about being late? You've missed at least five classes and you haven't given me the last paper.

MARY: I have it! I was up half the night to finish it...but I did it. *(Holds essay out to* WILLOW*.)*

WILLOW: I wish I could help you, Mary, but that paper will not get you any marks. It's too late. The reality is that you aren't going to make this class. I'm sorry. You've just missed too much.

MARY: You can't do that! I'm trying... you can't just throw my work away like it's garbage.

WILLOW: Listen, Mary. I really like you. I do. Honestly, you have the ability to go a lot further in University. You have the writing skills, the reasoning, the insight... but it doesn't mean a damn thing if you don't hand in your assignments.

It's not fair to the other students. Just because I'm Indian doesn't mean you can do your work any time you want. We're trying to beat these stereotypes and we're not going to do it with your attitude...not on your life! *(Calms down.)* This is just one class. There are other classes you can take next semester.

MARY: There won't be any more semesters. I've had it with you people. You don't understand.

WILLOW: Mary! You give me poetry when I need an essay. This is a University.... You have to write essays with footnotes and sources.... You have to play their game.

MARY: Have it your way, you fucking bitch. I don't need you or anybody else...

WILLOW: Okay, look, I think it's time we talked. I have a friend you might feel more comfortable with.

MARY: A friend?

WILLOW: Well, he's a counsellor, a real nice guy...

MARY: *(Exploding.)* None of you care! How could you? I hate you! Do you know what it's like to be alone? Do you? I don't have anybody! All I have is a picture of my mom.... *(Breaks down.)* That's all I have... *(MARY starts to leave. WILLOW trys to stop her. MARY viciously pulls away.)* Get your hands off me! Do you hear me, Miss Apple? Just fuck off!

(MARY exits, WILLOW stand speechless, lights down.)

Scene X – Suicide

MAHKÊSÎS: *tânisi,* again out there, my brothers and sisters. This is the fox here again on CHIP 90.5 FM.... Unfortunately I don't feel too frisky this morning...I think about growing up in a small town in Northern Saskatchewan and going to Main Street on Saturday night and standing outside the bar listening to my relatives and friends and people I knew drinking themselves silly. Of course we only really heard the laughter...the good times. *(Lights up on woman drinking in the bar with a Bohemian beer.)* But I'll never forget this old lady with a scarf around her head holding on to her lonely Bohemian beer...and her sad eyes staring at nothing.... That same song was on the jukebox...some ol' tearjerker by ol' Hank Williams...So I thought I'd dig it up and play it for you.... I hope you don't mind.... It's just the mood ol' Mahkêsîs is in this morning.... For my brother.... *(Song begins, continues for a couple spins, then we hear a scratch as the song is removed suddenly.)* Naw,...changed my mind.... Sorry, Hank.... But I'll tell you...enough is enough...I'm gonna play my brother's favorite song... 'cause that's what he'd want.... He loved to party.... Here it is.... That's right ... Ernie is back.. Ernest Moonias and the Shadows with...look out... "Devil's on the Loose".... Go get 'em Ernie.... This is Red Skies and this is CHIP FM...90.5...and that's no jive... *(Song begins, lights down.)*

(Lights up on MARY standing on the street with her shopping cart.)

VOICE: Whhoooooeeee! Hey, honey, how about it?

MARY: How about what?

VOICE: You know what I want...just a little bit of candy.

MARY: Fuck off!...just fuck off!

(Three masked figures come in, one holding a whisky bottle, another a vial of pills, another a huge razor blade. They dance and mime a panhandler, a drunk on the street, another passed out puking. They fight each other in a theatrical dance. MARY watches.)

MARY: I need something...I need something. Can you help me?

MAN #1: I got what you need, baby, a little bit of whisky.

MARY: I'll take it. Give it to me.

Man #2: Give me some money, Mary,...then you can have it.

Mary: OK, OK. I'm looking for my mom. Have you seen her?

(Man #1 puts the bottle on the sidewalk, laughs. Mary timidly picks the bottle up, holds it like a baby. Man #2 with the vial of pills begins to shake the pills in a bizarre rhythm.)

Mary: What's that?

Man #2: This is all you need, Mary... *(Keeps shaking the pills.)*

Mary: Will it work?

Man #2: *(Laughs)* You never know, Mary.... Check it out.

Mary: Give it to me.

Man #2: You got it, Mary, just slide me some green.... Didja cash your cheque?

Mary: Yeah, sure I did.

(Man #2 tosses Mary the pills, keeps dancing. Mary catches the pills, turns and sees the figure with the razor blade mime slashing up.)

Mary: What are you doing?

Man #3: Don't play dumb, Mary, you remember me.

Mary: Get away from me.

Man #3: It's kinda messy, Mary, but it works... *(Pretends to die.)*

Mary: Fuck off, all of you, just fuck offffff!

(Figures laugh, do a goodbye step and run away. Mary walks to a place, takes a blanket from her shopping cart and descends to the riverbank. Lights go down momentarily and come up on her sitting on the blanket with the shopping cart tipped over on its side. She is drinking straight from the bottle, with the picture of her mother in her hand.)

Mary: How can they talk to me like that? Like I'm dirt...Mother...Mom...can you hear me? Why the fuck is this happening to me? Why? Why? Goddamn you, Mom! Why did you leave me? I was just a baby! I hate you! Do you hear me, mom? I hate you ! These people in this city are cruel...they don't understand...they laugh at me like I'm not right...is that what it was like for you, Mom? Did people ever laugh at you? *(Lights come up on woman with back to audience sitting at a bar table with one draft.)*

Oh God...that brings us back to here, Mom, home sweet home...now all I have to do is go through the motions, and maybe, who knows, I'll run into you down the road, eh Mom? We can go over old times. You know, how you left me to fend for myself and I didn't make it. Maybe we can cry in each other's arms.... I'm sorry, baby. I hope you'll forgive me... *(She begins to swallow the pills and wash it down with the whisky.)*

It's so beautiful here.... Hey, river...always going somewhere...leaving me behind.... Do you hear me river? You just go where you're going and don't you worry about me...don't you worry about me....

(Dene Man appears above her. He is struggling with what he sees. He looks at her with pity and slowly turns and walks away, lights down. Lights come up on Maggie beading a moss bag. She peers into the night. Lights come up on Mary, comatose on the ground. The empty bottle is lying on the ground with the empty vial. Lights come up on Mary's empty bed, and then come up on Maggie, standing, holding the mossbag tightly. She turns and walks over to the radio and turns it on.)

(We hear the sounds of the Unceded Band with their offering, "Breathing Through my Gills." Music becomes background as Mahkêsîs breaks through.)

Mahkêsîs: Man, oh, man, that makes me feel...well, kinda sad, but happy.... Whodat?.... It's me, darlings, Mahkêsîs. I'm back in town and I've got the blues.... Tonight is, well,...one of those nights. I'm thinking about this woman right now...thinking about the way she talked and sighed and loved...and now she's gone.... Left me at twilight.... I remember the moment so well.... Here's a little blues for you, honey,...wherever you are.... Mahkêsîs will find you.... This is Red Skies on your dial, the mood of the night, the music of the spirit.... 90.5 on your dial...CHIP FM.... Saskatoon...

(Music swirls into the soundscape of drums, chants. Blackout.)

Scene XI – Hospital

(Light up on MARY who is swirling and dancing amidst a soundscape of drums, Dene, Cree and English voices meshing, electric guitar, thunder, and a statiky MAHKÊSÎS's voice occasionally breaking through. The Beatles' "Hey Jude", latin chants from a catholic mass juxtapose. Figures appear among the swirling MARY who is moving in a modern dance, and then the sound changes to a traditional Dene dance with the soundscape in the background pulsating in volume. The figures are in black with half masks, dancing until they begin to form a circle with MARY joining.)

MARY: Who are you?

WOMAN #1: I'm your mom, baby, don't you remember calling me?

MARY: Mom? Mommm?

WOMAN #1: SSShhhh... sssh... child.... Just dance... I'm just learning too.

MARY: Where am I?

WOMAN #1: I hear I'm gonna be a grandma, Mary? For God's sake, I'm too young to be a *kôkom*...

MARY: What?

MAN #1: You're with your people, Mary,.... I'm your father, Jerome. I never met you.

MARY: My dad?...Mom! Mom! *Ene! Ene!* Is that true?

MAN #1: She's gone, Mary,.... But it's true.... I never meant to leave you.... I hope you're not mad at me.

MARY: I'm not mad...I'm just...I don't know. Please help me. I don't like this.

MAN #1: SSShhhhh...girl...let's just dance. All your relatives are here...dancing with you.... There's your Auntie Bella and your Uncle Edward.... Wave at them or something. Boy, you're ignorant.

MARY: Who? I don't know anybody in my family. *(Spots another woman.)* Who the hell are you?

WOMAN #2: I'm your grandmother, Mary, I'm Delores, the good looking one...*(Chuckle.) glah na tehl...glah na tehl... (The words begin to echo from the speakers.)*

MARY: Where's Mom? And that guy...*Seta?*...Dad?

WOMAN #3: They went back home...hungry from all that dancing...I guess you're coming home, too, my girl.... Finally...back to Patuanak.

MARY: I don't have a home...did you hear me? *(Begins to panic.)* Oh, shit...I remember now...I took those pills... *(She breaks the circle and falls, she sees blood on her dress and screams, the figures surround her, she gets up again.)* AAAmm I dead? AAAm I? I don't want to die! *(Grabs her stomach.)* My babbbbyyyy!

(MARY is crying uncontrollably. The figures stop dancing, bend over to touch and console her, and then melt away.)

MARY: Momm? Mom?

(Blackout to hospital bed. Lights change to a hospital aura. MARY is in a bed, intravenous tubes running into her hand. She is in a sitting position. Suddenly she jerks awake, not knowing where she is and, then she

remembers the baby, touches her stomach and visibly relaxes.)

MARY: Dear God, please understand, I felt so lonely...I didn't know what I was doing.... *(Starts sobbing softly.)*

(MAGGIE enters the room quietly from the half-open door. She hears the sobs and stops just beyond the door not wanting to startle MARY)

MAGGIE: Don't cry, my girl, it'll be okay.

MARY: *(Surprised and relieved.)* Oh Maggie.... *(Maggie comforts her.)* Am I alive? Do you know if my baby's OK?

MAGGIE: The baby's fine...don't you worry...it's over....

MARY: How did you know how to find me? I'm so ashamed, Maggie.... I just.... *(Breaks down again.)*

(MAGGIE cradles MARY in her arms, rocking her like a baby. Time passes.)

MARY: Maggie...I'm not strong like you.... I felt like I was suffocating or something. I just wanted to go to sleep and forget about everything...helpless...helpless....

MAGGIE: Mary, I can't help you if you don't want me to...you tell me what's bothering you when you're ready, OK?

MARY: I know...but it's so hard...Maggie...I'm going to have a baby.

MAGGIE: I know....I'm happy for you...you'll be a good mother.

MARY: You must think I'm some kind of a monster or something.... I just couldn't stand it anymore.... I just couldn't stand it.

MAGGIE: It's hard to understand, Mary,...but you're in good hands now.... I think you have a visitor downstairs waiting to see you.... He's been here since yesterday...a nice guy...and he's an Indian even.

MARY: A man? What does he want?

MAGGIE: To see you, stupid. *(They both begin to laugh.)*

MARY: Who is he?

MAGGIE: Beats me. But he sure is anxious to see you.

MARY: I don't know any men....Tell him I've got to sleep.

MAGGIE: OK, but he's not bad looking for somebody that's been awake for 24 hours.... I think he said his name is Joe.... He met you at the dumpster... *(Laughs)*

MARY: *(Remembering.)* Oh, shit...I remember.... I think I puked on him....What's he doing here... how?...

MAGGIE: He carried you to the hospital, Mary,...he seen your shopping cart down by the bridge.... *(Pause.)* I'll tell him you need some rest.... He's waited this long, he'll come back tomorrow.

MARY: He carried me here? I don't even know him. Does he know I've got a bannock in the oven?

MAGGIE: *(Laughs.)* I'll leave now. Take it easy. I'll see you soon *(Hugs.)* Remember: No dancing and no hickies. *(Exits.)*

(Lights down.)

Scene XII – Bridge

(WILLOW is running with her walkwoman. MAGGIE is standing on the bridge looking into the water. WILLOW runs past MAGGIE, then stops, removes her headphones. She walks over to MAGGIE tentatively.)

WILLOW: Are you Maggie?

Maggie: That's me. You must be Willow.

Willow: Yes....the teacher...Native Studies Department.

Maggie: *ânîn* Willow from the Native Studies Department.

Willow: Mary...Mary of Patuanak. I heard she had an accident.

Maggie: Yes, it's true. She's at the University Hospital. I just came from there.

Willow: How is she?

Maggie: She's gonna be all right...and the baby too.

Willow: She's pregnant? Oh, my God, I didn't know.

Maggie: I come here to watch the river. It's pretty this time of night. Sometimes you can see the whooping cranes feeding. Look. There they are.

Willow: Can she have visitors?

Maggie: You'd like to see her?

Willow: I could take her some flowers and fruit. Does she need anything?

Maggie: She needs to sleep without dreaming. *(Pause.)* I really like standing here when I need to think.

Willow: I was wondering what you were doing.

Maggie: She has a guy waiting for her.

Willow: That's nice. When are visiting hours?

Maggie: Where are you from, Willow?

Willow: Ontario.

MAGGIE: I went there, once. Niagara Falls.

WILLOW: I'm Mohawk.

MAGGIE: Have you ever been to Niagara Falls?

WILLOW: Yes, I have....listen, Maggie, what's wrong with that girl?

MAGGIE: I don't know, Willow, I just don't know.

WILLOW: *(Notices that MAGGIE has been crying.)* I'm sorry. I didn't realize.

MAGGIE: She's going back to Patuanak. *(Pause.)* If you're real quiet, you can walk by the river and catch *amisk* working...the beaver..over there. He's been busy. Do you see, Willow?

WILLOW: I see.

MAGGIE: How do you say *amisk* in your language?

WILLOW: I don't know. I never spoke it when I was a kid.

MAGGIE: Lots of us don't know our languages. You're not alone. I'm going down there on the riverbank to look for some roots. Do you want to come with me, Willow?

WILLOW: What do I do?

MAGGIE: Nothing. Just enjoy the river. I'll show you.

(They begin to walk toward the river.)

MAGGIE: Do they have wolves in Mohawk territory?

(They exit. Lights down.)

Trimester Two

Scene XIII – Night Zone

(In the dark we hear Robbie Robertson's "Somewhere Down the Crazy River." Lights gradually come up on a street scene. MARY is standing on a street corner on a lonely night with her shopping cart. The wind is blowing. She is mumbling a bit, trying to tune into something, perhaps in the wind, perhaps in the headphones she is wearing. JOE appears on the opposite end of the stage. He spots MARY.)

JOE: Mary, Mary, quite contrary...it's me...Joe. *(Stares at her for a long moment.)* What's wrong? You look like something's wrong.

MARY: *(Wearing a walkwoman, stares at JOE, forces a smile.)* No..... no. Nothing's wrong.

JOE: Well...good...good.... I've been watching for you.... I mean, you didn't say anything when you left...so I thought I'd look for you.

MAHKÊSÎS: ...Sometimes I feel the wind talking just a little bit y'know cooin' like a baby...

MARY: How'd you know where to find me?

JOE: *(Embarrassed.)* Well...I...I...followed you for a while that day you went for a walk...you remember. I hope you don't think I'm weird or something. I just wanted to make sure you would be all right.

MARY: I just want to be alone, Joe.

MAHKÊSÎS: ...I feel the sky I really do...it even hurts sometimes like it's too beautiful...

JOE: I think I'm in love with you, Mary.

MARY: *(Long pause.)* Why?

MAHKÊSÎS: ...that moment when you looked through the sky right at me...

JOE: I don't know. *(Looks at his shoes.)* How's the baby?

MARY: I don't know, either,...Joe.... Listen, I don't know if I want this.

JOE: Why? We're just beginning to get to know each other.

MARY: I'm scared, Joe. Something's happening to me.

(JOE moves to her, they embrace.)

JOE: What? What is it?

MARY: I just don't know...Joe...do you.... Will you meet me later.... Tonight? I want to tell you something.... A secret, OK? *(Laughs.)*

JOE: Uh.... A secret.... I mean, later. It's already after eleven. Where could we meet?

MARY: In a dream.

JOE: What? *(Starts to laugh, stops)* What?

MARY: I told you. It's a secret.

MAHKÊSÎS: ...listening to sweet blues by somebody that's gone now...from this world....

MARY: Well?

JOE: What do you mean, Mary?

MARY: I'm going to have a dream tonight and I want you to be...part of it.

JOE: *(Laughs nervously now.)* That's what I thought you said.

MARY: You think there's something wrong with me, don't you?

JOE: No...I...I...don't think there's anything wrong with... *(Breaks up laughing.)* ...I'm sorry. But you gotta admit it's a little spooky...I was hoping we could just go for...a pizza or something. *(Chuckles, sees MARY is silent.)* Sorry. Well OK, OK.... Tell me more.

MAHKÊSÎS: ...Hear the heartbeat...listen real hard...until you know for sure.

MARY: You've got to promise...

JOE: ...not to tell. Right?

MARY: Right.

JOE: So...what should I do?

MARY: There'll be somebody else there.

JOE: Huh?

MARY: In the dream...there'll be someone else there. But it's OK.

JOE: I hope so. Shit.

MARY: Good...good.

JOE: Uh...Mary...you're really serious about this, aren't you?

MARY: Listen, fuckhead, do you want to...or not?

JOE: I guess so. I mean, sure...as long as I don't have to miss work.... Oh, sorry. What shall I do? Is it a ceremony or something?

MARY: Oh. *(stares at JOE.)* Joe, you look lost. *(Walks over to him.)* Hey, I never noticed before. You've got shit-brown eyes.

(Takes his face in her hands and slowly, then passionately kisses him on the mouth. JOE is taken aback, MARY looks at him with amusement, puts her hand up to his cheek, and then deliberately slaps him just hard enough to make a smacking sound, but not hard enough to really hurt. JOE recoils with bewilderment. MARY laughs heartily, puts her headphones on, grabs her shopping cart and departs).

JOE: *(In a state of shock.)* Hey! I mean.... Hey!

MAHKÊSÎS: ...c'mon in, sit down..its gonna be a looong night....

(Music fades. Blackout.)

Scene XIV – Love

(Marvin Gaye's "Let's Get It On" is playing on the radio. Moans and groans, climax in the dark as lights fade. Lights come up with MARY smoking in bed, JOE gazing at her, lovestruck.)

JOE: Wow! I'm impressed! *(Kisses MARY.)*

MARY: I wish I could say the same.

JOE: *(Realization kicks in.)* My God! That was good! I love you, Mary.

(MARY caresses JOE, kisses him, they start to get passionate again, JOE stops.)

MARY: What's wrong?

JOE: I'm sorry...I just can't seem to get into it...too many things running around my head.

MARY: *(Lifts sheet.)* I see.

JOE: *(Laughs.)* Mary...Mary....You're strange. *(Reaches for his pants and takes out some pot, begins rolling a joint.)*

MARY: Is that dope?

JOE: Yeah.

MARY: Oh.

JOE: I hope you don't mind.

MARY: I guess not, if you don't mind strange women.

(JOE finishes rolling joint, lights it, has a toke, coughs.)

JOE: This should make things clearer... *(Chuckles.)* So.... Mary.... I...I... *(Kisses her.)* I hope it was OK for you.

MARY: It was wonderful. Thank you. Just leave the money on the counter.

JOE: *(Chuckles.)* Yeah! Wasn't it?

MARY *(Pause)* Why do you smoke that stuff?

JOE: I don't. It smokes me.... Ha Ha...beats drinking. You never smoked?

MARY: No.

JOE: Wanna try some?

MARY: What's it like?

JOE: It's great!...makes you laugh...forget about stuff y'know.

MARY: No, I better not.

JOE: Yeah... I forgot *(Sarcastic)* the baby *(Sees MARY is offended.)* Oh sorry. *(Silence, JOE has another toke.)* So why me?

MARY: Huh?

JOE: Why me?

MARY: *(Laughs.)* I like you...a lot. Even though I hardly know you.... It just seemed right somehow.

JOE: Actually Mary to tell you the truth...I'm honoured to be the one *(Kisses her.)*

MARY: I think I'm gonna get sick.

JOE: Please, not on me.

MARY: You're kinda goofy, aren't you?

JOE: Yup.

MARY: Well, actually, I'd like to try it sometime...just to see what happens.

JOE: Go ahead. Take a couple of hits. It's skunkweed.

MARY: What?

JOE: It's skunkweed.... High quality shit.

MARY: No, I'm not going to do it.

JOE: Hey, speaking of crazy shit... you were a little bizarre on the street when I caught up to you.

MARY: I...I...can't explain some things...sometimes.

JOE: Mary, what is going on here? We make love, you talk about dreamwalking.... Jeesus, I'm just a carpenter.

MARY: I don't want to be alone any more. Joe, I want you with me.

JOE: I want to be with you too.

(They kiss and lie there for a while.)

MARY: I'm too excited to sleep.

Joe: Me too...shouldn't have smoked that joint.

Mary: So what should we do? *(They look at each other and giggle and begin making love again. Isley Brothers cut in on the radio.)*

Mahkêsîs: AAAAhhhhhh! Didja you know about love? Indian love? We used to hide under a blanket in the old days and everybody knew we were sweet on each other. Remember those arranged marriages, boys? When I was in high school in North Battleford, there was this beautiful tall Cree woman from Saulteaux or Moosomin, I forget, and I guess she had to get married to some guy she didn't want. *tâpwê* boy. If she was still living in the old days all she'd have to do is get on her horse with the one she wanted and take off for a couple of days. When she came back the tribe just accepted it...that's the way love's gotta be...Hey, boys, when you're on that powwow trail, snagging, don't forget they call them hickies powwow stickers, and don't forget to take care of your babies nine months after.... Nowadays those runaway dads are all over, jumpin' and hollerin', partyin' like they don't got a care in the world, and back in the shack is their woman lookin' after their babies, stayin' up all night nursing their child while big Daddy is nursing a Budweiser. Don't it make you wanna scream! Go ahead! Let it all out!

(Music Fades. Blackout.)

Scene XV – Dream

(Lights up on Mary and Joe sleeping in her bed suspended in the air. We hear the Dene chant, some dream sequence music until Mary and Joe arise and meet in the dream world. They are wearing different clothes. Mary is wearing a business suit and heels, with her hair up. She is carrying a briefcase. Joe is dressed in traditional Cree clothing, circa 1830s. They look at each other for a long time. Dream sequence music plays throughout the scene in the background.)

Joe: Mary, is that you?

MARY: You're very perceptive, Joe.

JOE: Migawd, I can't believe this...is this actually happening.... We're meeting in a dream.... I can't believe it.

MARY: Thanks for believing in me, Joe.... That really means a lot.

JOE: *(Just notices his clothing.)* Hey! What the...! Where did I get this get-up? I look like Tonto, for Christ's sake.

MARY: You look great, Joe. All the women will want to beat me up.

JOE: Why? I mean...I do? I never really thought of myself as an....

MARY: An Indian, Joe?

JOE: Yeah, I guess so.

MARY: Well, how does it feel?

JOE: It feels good.... Except I'm a little spooked here...it's safe here, huh, Mary?

MARY: Of course.

JOE: So what next? What do we do now?

MARY: You got me. I just invited you to the dream. Anything can happen...anything. Just don't fuck it up.

JOE: Whooaa! Anything? Mary, you got to be kidding!

MARY: Do you have a smoke, Joe?

JOE: No, don't you remember? I don't smoke...just a little grass now and then.

MARY: Did you bring some?

Joe: Yeah, it's in my...oh shit...it's in my other pants.... These pants have no pockets.... Where did they put stuff?

Mary: What's that around your neck?

Joe: Huh? *(Looks at neck, discovers medicine bag.)* Hey! Wow! This is right out of the twilight zone.... It's a little leather bag.... Let me see... *(Opens Bag.)* Hhhmmmm.

Mary: So what is it?

Joe: *(Inspects bag further.)* It's a plant of some kind. *(Smells contents.)* ...I don't know...smells nice though.

Mary: Let me see. *(Smells.)* It's sweetgrass...you have your very own medicine bag.

(Opens her briefcase, extracts a huge joint, lights it.)

Joe: But I'm not sick...am I? Or does it matter? Oh shit! Get me out of here! *(Notices Mary smoking a huge joint.)* Hey! What do you think you're doing?

Mary: Getting high. *(Chokes and coughs.)* Geez, how do you do it?

Joe: Mary, get serious! You can't do that!

Mary: Why not? You do.

Joe: That's different! I'm not pregnant...oh shit...what about the baby? The baby, for God's sake?

Mary: *(Spots something happening.)* Hey! What's that? *(They look into the dream, further.)* ...In the bush...there...some people down there.

Joe: Looks like Indians. What are they doing? They're fighting.... Oh shit, they're coming this way.

(DENE warriors run through the dream, sounds of battle, men yelling,

etc. MARY and JOE cringe together, MARY continues to smoke the joint. DENE MAN from the dream appears. He sees MARY and JOE and stops.)

JOE: This must be your friend, Mary. Hi, I'm Joe. *(Extends hand to DENE. DENE MAN smiles.)* Great! I think we're going to hit it off, Mary. Hey, he's got a tooth missing.

MARY: Just wait till he finds out you're Cree...ooops!

(DENE MAN bristles and draws out his knife. He motions MARY away from JOE. She keeps puffing on the joint. He asks her something in Dene. She ignores him. The sound of battle dies and we hear birds singing.)

DENE MAN: *Yuwe nigha, ena, thebaigha.*

JOE: Oh, God, he's going to kill me! Do something, Mary! Answer him! Quick!

MARY: *(Really high.)* I don't understand him, man. Wait! Stop! Don't hurt him! See, he won't listen...

(MARY goes back to smoking joint. The DENE MAN looks momentarily confused and then attacks JOE with the knife. They grapple furiously. MARY throws down the joint and tries to hit the DENE MAN with her briefcase but they are moving too fast. It is a fight to the death.)

JOE: Oh fuck! This guy's nuts! Mary watch out!

(They grapple more, the DENE MAN is talking to MARY in a way that suggests that JOE is the enemy. Finally JOE wins the struggle and sits astride the man. JOE is about to plunge the knife into the DENE MAN when MARY begins to chant in Dene. All stop, transfixed, and listen. Song ends. They stare at MARY, and the doorbell rings.)

MARY: Joe, could you get that please?

JOE: What?

(MAGGIE enters carrying a bucket of Kentucky Fried Chicken, dressed

in KFC *delivery service clothes. She is not smiling)*

MAGGIE: That'll be $32.95.

MARY: Maggie, what are you doing?

MAGGIE: That'll be $33.95. Us elders got to pay our bills too.

MARY: But why didn't you tell me? Maybe I could have helped...

MAGGIE: *(Draws MARY close to her.)* Listen to me, Mary, and listen good. You have to take this power seriously. Do you hear me? This is not a game.

MARY: I didn't realize what was happening here. I didn't mean to do anything wrong.

JOE: *(DENE MAN mutters something angrily at JOE.)* Oh sorry. *(Gets off of man.)*

MARY: Joe, I think we better talk..

(As they stare at each other, DENE MAN stands and then pays MAGGIE for the chicken and walks away with MAGGIE, arm around her.)

JOE: What's happening, Mary? What's going on?

MARY: I think we better go home now.

JOE: Now? I was just starting to get used to this. This guy... *(Motions to where DENE MAN was, realizes he's gone.)* Shit...he split.... Hey! Where's my chicken?

MARY: Joe...it doesn't matter.

JOE: Who's that?

(FREDDIE enters pushing MARY's shopping cart filled with empty beer bottles.)

JOE: Hey! It's Freddie.... Hey, Fred. Glad you could make it.

FREDDIE: Many years I have felt the pain in my heart
Without love, without joy, without peace
Will I return to my home or shall I wander?

(JOE and MARY look at each other. FREDDIE sees the roach on the floor, picks it up, lights it, has a toke, spots JOE and MARY, winks. Lights darken. Lights up again on MARY and JOE in bed.)

MARY: *(Wakes Joe)* Are you alright, Joe?

(JOE says nothing, just sits staring at wall. Lights down.)

Scene XVI – Buds On Broadway

(Music comes up with the lights, "Ninety-Nine Pounds," by Jani Lauzon. We are at a bar with GEORGE, WILLOW and KENNY sitting at a high table with bar stools. Three empty beer pitchers and an overflowing ashtray decorate the table. They are all 'high' on alcohol. Lights also come up on JOE and FREDDIE at another table. They are also drinking, FREDDIE, a Bud and JOE, a Coke. Waitress returns to GEORGE'S table with another full pitcher.)

KENNY: So what about this trip, Prof? When's the stagecoach leaving?

GEORGE: When the details are taken care of Willow, tell me more about this woman, Mary.

WILLOW: I believe she could be the key, Professor. She's going back to Patuanak and she is Dene. Maybe it'll work.

GEORGE: We need somebody to gain some access to this tight circle. They don't trust any outsiders. I wonder if somehow we could join her?

WILLOW: I understand the community is recreating their traditional homes before contact, and then they'll have the ceremony. If we're not invited, we had better be prepared to make an offering, gentlemen.

KENNY: You mean, a stipend? *(Laughs.)*

GEORGE: How much, Willow?

WILLOW: We're not talking about money, we're talking about traditional gifts, cloth, tobacco...something important to you...something sacred.

KENNY: *(Laughs.)* Hey George, looks like you're going to have to give up that twenty-year-old bottle of scotch you got stashed away.

WILLOW: Shut up, Kenny.

(Segue to JOE and FREDDIE.)

JOE: I'm worried about you.

FREDDIE: Don't worry about me, just worry about yourself.

JOE: I heard you're into the coke.

FREDDIE: Who told you that?

JOE: Never mind. Are you or aren't you?

FREDDIE: Who was it?.... It was Cindy who told you, right?

JOE: I don't know no Cindy.... C'mon Freddie, stop bullshitting me.

FREDDIE: OK, OK, So I've done a couple lines here and there. Big fucking deal.

JOE: You're gonna lose your job if you mess with the blow.

FREDDIE: Who are you, my dad?

JOE: No...just a friend.... Just a friend.

(Segue to GEORGE *and* WILLOW *and* KENNY.*)*

GEORGE: Believe it or not, according to this legend, it's supposed to happen in conjunction with the aurora borealis.

KENNY: That's totally mystical, sir.

WILLOW: Kenny, will you stop!

KENNY: Well...shit.... Suppose my stars are lined up someday. *(Breaks up laughing.)*

GEORGE: Leave him be, Willow. He'll pay for it tomorrow.

KENNY: What's that supposed to mean?

WILLOW: You mean to tell me that the Northern Lights play a part in this too?

GEORGE: It's really not my realm of expertise. I'm more than a little perplexed.

WILLOW: I'm going to do some more research on the Dene.... Sounds fascinating.

KENNY: Hey, I'm talking to you, Professor.

(Segue to FREDDIE *and* JOE.*)*

JOE: Do you ever dream, Freddie?

FREDDIE: What kinda question is that?

JOE: Well, do you?

FREDDIE: You mean, like dreaming to be Axel Rose or something?

JOE: No...just to dream, you know...a simple dream.

FREDDIE: Yeah. Yeah. I think so. *(Pause.)* Hey! Once I dreamed I was giving it to Madonna. But she farted, man.

JOE: You're a sick man, Freddie.... A sick man.

(Segue to GEORGE, etc.)

GEORGE: I think I'm ready for home, friends.

KENNY: Ya giving up boss?

GEORGE: No, I'm not giving up. I've just had enough of this piss beer and enough of your ignorant babble.

WILLOW: C'mon, you two...this is so stupid.

KENNY: Well,...Christ...Willow, are you sticking up for this bigot...he's cutting down our people.

GEORGE: Look here, asshole...I simply said that we introduced a new way of life to you people that's probably better in the long run.

KENNY: Aw, fuck....you said you were Lake Superior or something.

WILLOW: C'mon Kenny, you're drunk. Let's get you home.

KENNY: Why don't you go home? Me and the prof have some business here.

WILLOW: Why don't you fuck off?

(Segue to JOE and FREDDIE)

JOE: I was looking for some tipi poles, if you must know.

FREDDIE: Holy Shit!... If I didn't hear it with my own ears, I wouldn'ta believed it.

JOE: What?

FREDDIE: That woman's got you going back to the bush, ain't she?

JOE: So what.... It's quiet out there, a guy can think. I'm learning how to put up a tipi for the summer.... It'll be beautiful.

FREDDIE: Pretty soon you'll be sending up smoke signals and chasing buffalo around. *(Laughs.)*

JOE: How would you know, man? You're Indian, too, and you don't give a flying fuck.

FREDDIE: Fuck that shit, man.

JOE: Why are you so down on Indians, man?

FREDDIE: Fuck that shit, man. *(Pause.)* I'm not down on them.... Hey, have you ever seen them hanging out at the liquor store...man, that's pathetic.

JOE: Yeah.

FREDDIE: Which reminds me, pal, you should have a talk with your poor girlfriend...buy her a car or something.

JOE: Why? What are you talking about?

FREDDIE: That shit ass shopping cart she pushes around downtown. She looks like a bag lady or something.

JOE: There's nothing wrong with someone pushing a shopping cart around. *(Pause.)* She says it makes her humble.

FREDDIE: Fuckkk.

(Lights up on MARY with shopping cart. She is wearing a business dress and mukluks.)

MARY: .... We cannot see the pain in their innocent eyes and their sweet whispers. They make us cry without knowing why; if only we could offer more than our skies and our animal skins to your faraway queens and kings. Joe? Joe!

(Segue to bar with JOE and FREDDIE)

JOE: She's really something special, Freddie...she makes me feel...high!

FREDDIE: Ha, Ha, fooled you, fooled you... you're already high.

JOE: Shut the fuck up, willya.... Geez.

(Segue to GEORGE and WILLOW.)

GEORGE: Do you think I'm a racist boor too?

WILLOW: No...just a boor...just kidding, George. Are you sure you want another drink?

(Segue to MAGGIE dancing to Billy Preston's "Outa Space".)

MAGGIE: ...*pêyak*...*nîso*...*nisto*....*nêwo*...and that's a *niyânan*... and *nikotwâsik* and a *têpakohp*....

(Continues to dance, music, lights go down, segue to JOE and FREDDIE.)

FREDDIE: Can you buy me a beer? I'm getting a little tapped out.

JOE: You're always tapped out.

FREDDIE: That's what I like about you, Joe. You're so fucking.... So fucking....

JOE: Spit it out, Fred.

FREDDIE: So fucking tight.

JOE: Yeah, right.

FREDDIE: Please, man. Five bucks.

JOE: Why do I bother?

FREDDIE: Because you love me.

(Segue to GEORGE and KENNY grappling on the floor, WILLOW and the waitress trying to break them up.)

WILLOW: Stop it, you fucking idiots...they're phoning the cops.... Get off of him, George,...fuckkkk!

(Segue to MAGGIE, dancing hard now.)

MAGGIE: *ayênânêw...kêkâ....mi...tâ...taht......mi...tâ......taht..... a...tat....a ...tat...tat.*

(All freeze as MARY walks through with her shopping cart.)

MARY: ...And when the red sun climbed slowly in the east,
Was I not there to greet you in a good way?
Did I not dance with great happiness with my children?
These things are unknown to me...they are lost
Forever...forever.

MAHKÊSÎS: Saturday night in "Toon town"...ya gotta love it...and I hope you are all having big fun out there tonight on the prairies. But there's always a reason to celebrate...so how does Mahkêsîs celebrate? Well, the ol' fox likes to get down too, but had to give up those...substances, if you know what I mean, and what about you? What do you like? Whatever it is, don't overdo it. Remember to keep everything in balance...the medicine wheel is turning...which way is it turning for you?...ha...it's Red Skies on your dial 90.5 FM...the beat of the street and the sound of the city.... Ho, let's keep it going with, you guessed it, CCR with a dedication to the boys from Green town,...rowdyville and the sounds of Green River.... I can hear the bullfrogs callin' me now.... Yeahh...

(Creedence breaks in nice and loud. Lights down.)

Scene XVII – MAGGIE's Circle

(Lights up on MAGGIE sitting in her chair at home with a cup of tea.)

MAGGIE: I only ask that we respect what we are learning and to show respect to those who teach us...but to remember that we are human beings who will always make mistakes. There was a Cree woman I knew who was making a dress for her daughter. It was a special dress for her wedding, a traditional wedding. She worked for months on that dress, cleaning the deer hide herself and carefully sewing that dress with love and patience. And the beadwork was so beautiful, Woodland Cree design with the flowers and the leaves, you know the kind they make. Anyways, one day she finally finished and she showed the dress to her daughter. Her daughter was so happy when she saw the dress her eyes were just shining. She was looking at the beadwork and she saw one tiny bead that was sewn into the design that was the wrong colour.

(WILLOW walks in and stands listening.)

She didn't know what to say to her mother, because she knew she worked so hard on that dress. But she couldn't help herself, and she finally said, "Mom, look...there's one bead here that's the wrong colour. Her mother just looked at her and smiled, and said, "I sewed that one bead there so the Creator would know I'm not perfect. I'm just a human being." *(Pause.)* Oh hello, hello, *ânîn*.... I'm so glad you could come.

WILLOW: I'm sorry...I'm very late...that's a beautiful story.

MAGGIE: Are you hungry?

WILLOW: No, I'm OK. Maggie, can you wait a minute? I...I have to tell you something. It's the sweat lodge.... I've been to one before...in Akwesasne.... But I chickened out.

MAGGIE: When you're ready, you'll know it.

WILLOW: There's something else. It's George and Kenny, the guys I work with. I don't know if I should be with them. I got this feeling that George is using us to get some information on a ceremony up North.... And Kenny is so disrespectful.... I'm kinda caught in the middle. We're going up there... to Patuanak. I'm scared and I don't know why.

MAGGIE: Those people are very powerful...those Dene. It'll be good to meet them.

WILLOW: Mary's involved.

MAGGIE: Mary?

WILLOW: Yes. I told them I knew her and they think she can help them...find this ceremony...oh, shit,...I don't know what's going on.

MAGGIE: Willow, will you join us?

WILLOW: I feel like a stranger.

MAGGIE: Come. The women are waiting for us.

(MAGGIE puts her arm around WILLOW. They walk into the meeting room. Lights down, music from the Dakota nation fills the room.)

MAHKÊSÎS: Well Well Well... isn't that pretty? That's a Dakota group from Moose Woods with our own little version of "Silent Night"...speakin' of...we'll be celebratin' Christmas very soon. I hope you're ready to eat a lot a grub and see old friends and relatives. This is the time to renew all those friendships, a time to bury the hatchet with your mother-in-law and to go broke finding those Christmas presents. Sharing has been part of our traditions for as long as we can remember when we travelled this land in search of the buffalo, elk, moose or deer. We always made sure the poorest families had some meat in their pot... a time to stick together and survive and be strong.... This is the fox, Mahkêsîs, on a snowy night in December, wishing you and yours all the best.... I love you... *kisâkihitin*... honest! Ha!

(Song continues to play and fades out.)

TRIMESTER THREE

Scene XVIII – River

(MARY and JOE are making their way down to the riverbank. It is slippery, as it is December.)

JOE: Mary, I love you but what the hell are we doing down here?

MARY: I have to come down here, Joe. It's important. Watch it.

JOE: Yeah, but you're as big as a house. This is stupid. You could fall and hurt yourself. *(JOE falls.)* Shit! See what I mean!

MARY: You're OK?

JOE: What's so important down here?

MARY: Oh Joe, I have the best news to tell you. I went to the sweat lodge with Maggie and it was incredible. I could feel the baby moving and, oh.... I don't know how to describe it.

JOE: Isn't it a little hot in there?... a little dangerous, perhaps?

MARY: You know I wouldn't put our baby in danger, Joe.

JOE: Yeah, I know that.

MARY: Well, we're here. Sit.

JOE: In the snow?

MARY: Don't be that way. Here...I have something. *(Pulls a blanket from her knapsack.)* Sit. I've got some wood. We can make a fire.

JOE: No, it's OK. It's real warm here. Strange.

MARY: *(Sits beside JOE)* You probably think I'm nuts, huh, Joe? Sitting here on the riverbank in December.

JOE: Nothing surprises me anymore. Hey, look at the view...the reflection of the ice.

MARY: There's the Bessborough. And you can just see the statue of Gabriel Dumont....

JOE: You come here by yourself, don't you?

MARY: Don't get mad, Joe. There's absolutely nobody here in the winter and I just love it. I build a fire and pretend I'm Mary, Spirit of the River People.

JOE: Nobody ever bothers you?

MARY: No. Just me and the river.

JOE: It is nice here.... I never thought about coming down here in the winter.

MARY: Oh, there's animals that come here too...tracks all over...deer, beaver, fox, badger...all kinds.

JOE: I like it.

MARY: Listen, Joe. Quick, put your head here. Can you feel the baby moving?

(JOE puts his head on her stomach)

JOE: No...just a minute.... Ssshh.... Oh yes, now I hear.... It's moving now...wow!

MARY: I wonder if the baby knows where it is...sorta?

JOE: Beats me. Nice and warm down here. I'm staying.

(Time passes.)

Mary: Joe, I want to go back to Patuanak.

Joe: I knew you were gonna say that.

Mary: I want to go tomorrow.

Joe: I said we're going there anyways, but tomorrow...c'mon. *(Silence.)* The baby's due in a couple of weeks. We shouldn't even be down here.

Mary: I want to have the baby in Patuanak, Joe.

Joe: Absolutely not.

Mary: Look at the stars, Joe...they're telling you something.

Joe: There's no hospitals there.

Mary: You know what the Cree word for star is?

Joe: We don't have good tires.

Mary: It's *acâhkos*.... Nice, huh?

Joe: We don't know anybody there.

Mary: Joe, you're going to be a great father.

Joe: I know.

Mary: ....the world at her moccasined feet and a bird singing in her heart. *Glah na tehl.*

(Lights down.)

Scene XIX – Blue Angel

("Blue Angel" by Incognito breaks into the soundscape, volume increasing and then levelling off. Lights up on Maggie driving to Patuanak, humming along. Lights up on wise ones, Willow at the wheel, George and Kenny sleeping on each other. Mahkêsîs comes on with music in background.

MAHKÊSÎS: Here's a Métis blues howler from North Battleford, Saskatchewan, who hitchhiked to Chicago in the seventies with bells on his bell-bottoms just to learn how to blow those blues away. His name is Sherman Doucette and he's coming right at ya tonight on Red Skies. Speaking of howling the blues, we got a big ol' storm coming in from the North bringing with it lots of white stuff this holiday season...*kôna*...snow. Make sure you're ready for this storm, and if you're driving, I'm praying that you're doing fine...in Saskatoon it's a steady minus five, so it's not too too bad.... It's storytelling time in the lodges...so let's get out those stories and legends and keep those cultures warm.... In the meantime...you just relax and let Sherman drive this baby into your heart....This is the Fox and this is the sound of Saskatoon, CHIP 90.5...

(Song continues, lights down.)

Scene XX – Inn

(JOE and MARY are standing outside, arguing.)

JOE: I can't believe that asshole, Mary.... I can't believe it!... I'm going back in there!

MARY: Listen to me, Joe. It won't do any good.

JOE: I don't give a fuck.... How dare he say that stuff about us!

MARY: Joe, please....

JOE: I knew this was gonna happen. These people are racist up here. I could charge him for something.... Human rights violation or something. Damn!

MARY: Let's get in the truck, please.

JOE: You can back me up, Mary. I phoned and reserved a room for us...and then when we got here, he suddenly has no rooms.... It's because we're Indians! You know it!

Mary: We can't do anything about it now, Joe.

Joe: Bullshit. I'm going back in there.

Mary: He'll call the cops, Joe.

Joe: I don't give a shit who he calls...just wait here.

Mary: I know a place we can go, Joe.

Joe: What? That was the last motel, Mary.

Mary: I'll be right back. Don't go anywhere.

(Exits. Lights down, lights up on MAGGIE's car, she is humming along to Maggie Poochay's chant coming over the radio. MARY is standing on a desolate, windy road. Snow is blowing and the wind is picking up. She is wearing a light windbreaker and knee high wraparounds. Her dress is a coloured print reminiscent of the fifties. The sun is coming up and is painting the sky brilliant hues of purple and pink.)

Mary: Oh, Jesus...I can't believe this! I'm gonna freeze out here! Oh Mary, Mary, how could you be so stupid? You couldn't just sit in the truck and be warm and comfortable. Oh, God, Joseph is going to kill me for getting into this situation. That's if I don't die first. He'll probably thaw me out when he finds me just to give me shit. *(Looks around, takes stock of the situation.)* Well, Mary, it doesn't look like many folks are going to be travelling down this backroad on Sunday morning, in a blizzard to boot. Just my luck. Oh I'm so sorry, baby, I really didn't see this coming. I've got to think. What would Maggie do? God, Mary, you're so stupid. Maggie would be at home sleeping. What did our people do when they were caught in a storm? I know. They dug into the snow or something. That's what I'll do. Shit! I don't even have any gloves. They're still in the damn truck. Damn it all anyways. Mary, I wonder what it's like to freeze. They say that you get all warm just before you die. I wonder how they would know? Who are they anyways? Oh shit, I'm babbling again. At least my tongue won't freeze. Maggie!

Joseph! Help me! *(Pause.)* I think it's time for a prayer. Yes, that's what Maggie would say. Pray. *(A silent prayer issues from her lips.)* You know, God, even if I was to die out here it sure is a beautiful morning. I can see why the elders say you are the one that makes all things beautiful...*Sinire horelya horelya.*

(Time passes, MARY sinks down into the snow, she remains that way for a short time and then the DENE MAN appears. He goes to her and puts his hand on her shoulder.)

DENE MAN: *Kozigal... `sekwi degai hi nigha ha...uh huh...*

(MARY puts her hand in his and they disappear into the bush. Lights down)

Scene XXI – MAGGIE's Car

(Lights up on MAGGIE driving to Patuanak. She is singing a traditional song to herself as the windshield wipers keep their beat. Lights down on MAGGIE. Lights come up on WILLOW, GEORGE and KENNY in their vehicle driving to Patuanak. Lights down. Song that MAGGIE is singing continues in background.)

Scene XXII – JOE Blue

(JOE is standing outside in the storm looking extremely worried. He paces for awhile, straining to look into the failing light.

JOE: Where the hell is she? Damn...damn.... Well, I don't know what the hell to do... *(Sinks to his knees in the snow.)* I wish I believed in something...I could pray...sure that's what I could do...well, I guess you don't really have to believe in anything to pray, do you? God, Joseph, old boy, you should hear yourself.... You're going crazy, sure as shit.... Oh well, there's only the animals out here that are listening...they won't tell anybody.... Well here goes. *(Bows his head.)* Dear whoever.... This is Joseph talking here in the middle of nowhere.... I don't really believe in you but I don't want you to take it personal okay.... It's just that I have to talk to somebody...Mary's out there somewhere and she's going to have the baby any time now.... I feel like shit, man.... Seriously, man, can you do something about looking after her, because I feel hopeless.... Besides I'm from Saskatoon and I don't know anything about the bush. I couldn't tell the difference between a wolf track and a tractor track...well, maybe not that bad.... Honest, whoever you are, you will help me won't you? I tried to follow her tracks but they just disappeared like aliens got her or something. Aw shit I don't know what I'm saying anymore.... I don't know who's crazier, me for letting her go, or her for going.... I just want her and the baby to be okay...please...even though you know this isn't a real prayer...

(JOE gets off the ground, looks around, remembers his medicine bag. He removes it from his neck and holds it to the sky.)

This bag was given to me to protect me...in a dream...but I want to know if it'll protect you too, Mary, wherever you are.... I love you so much and I want to take care of you and the baby.... God....*kihci-manitow*...or whoever you are that won't talk...I really really care.... *(Long pause.)* You know, Joseph, you old pagan, I've never seen those lights look so bright.

(Northern Lights erupt. Wild moon music breaks in.)

Scene XXIII – Birth

(Lights up on MARY in pain walking toward a Dene lean-to with the DENE MAN. MAGGIE is standing at the lean-to wearing traditional clothing. Quickly, they lay MARY down on some furs and give her a birthing stick. She is very close to giving birth. The DENE MAN begins to beat the drum as a heartbeat, and then softly chants.)

MAGGIE: Mary, take it easy, girl...Maggie's here.

MARY: Well here we go, baby, you and me against the world. I don't know where you're coming from but I wish you'd hurry up *(Groan.)* ...Oh baby, baby, I love you.

(Lights up on WILLOW, GEORGE and KENNY looking at a map on the hood of a truck.)

WILLOW: You donkeys are not going to find this road on this map...Kenny?

KENNY: Jeezus, Willow...I was a little drunk that night.

WILLOW: I wish I knew something about the bush.... I feel like I'm a baby out here.

GEORGE: OK enough fraternizing, you two...my judgement's pretty hazy too, but I seem to.... *(Looks at the road.)* ...There! I think the trail's just over there.

WILLOW: Really?

GEORGE: Yup, I'm pretty sure.

KENNY: George used to be a moose hunter once upon a time.... Hey, George.

WILLOW: Really?

GEORGE: The James Bay Cree adopted me when I was a kid, at least for summer camp.... I spent a lot of time on the trapline.

WILLOW: *(Impressed.)* George, you never told me that. I thought you were...ah...

GEORGE: A stuffy upper class white kid with no idea....

WILLOW: Well.... Yeah.

KENNY: Well, you are stuffy..... *(They all laugh.)*

Willow: Mary's here somewhere. I can feel it...

Kenny: Look... the storm stopped.

George: Isn't that something?

Willow: Don't ask me how, guys...but I think Mary's at that Dene home...

George: In the storm?

Willow: I don't know, George. Damnit...let's find her.

Kenny: Wow!

(Segue to Mary.)

Mary: Oh, God, this hurts. Baby's...baby's coming to town.... Breathe...breathe...c'mon Mary. *(Screams.)*

(Segue to Joe.)

Joe: What was that? Mary? Mary? *(Begins to run toward the scream and freezes.)*

(Lights up on a transistor radio sitting outside Dene home.)

Mahkêsîs: Beautiful night for a celebration...wouldn't you say? AAAhh, I remember when I was a kid, I'd strap on my snowshoes and go cruising through the snow. The moon would make the snow dazzle and my breath would make cool patterns in the sky, and then I'd get lost. *(Chuckle.)* It's that time of year again, my brown friends, Christmas, that old Christian tradition ritual we've adopted over time..a time to think about our old ways..how we always share, help each other out. And again, this time, we need each other even more. Lots of kids don't have no presents under the tree. Remember these kids and help them out...something to make those kids eyes shine just like the snow...

(Segue to MARY)

MARY: Oh Goooooooddddd!.....Joseph! (Starts to sing in Dene.)

(Segue to JOE.)

JOE: Mary, where are you!?

(Segue to MAGGIE, who stands abruptly, shifts to MARY again, then to GEORGE, WILLOW and KENNY driving.)

GEORGE: So I think that native spirituality is still alive and well in some areas but I'm uncertain about the future.

WILLOW: Spirituality doesn't die, Professor.

KENNY: For some of us it does, Willow.

WILLOW: You don't believe in anything, Kenny?

(Segue to JOE stumbling on to the Dene home.)

JOE: Mary, are you all right?... Maggie...where the hell did you come from?

GEORGE: Well, Willow, I wasn't thinking that spirituality would die...possibly the rituals and ceremonies would become obsolete.

WILLOW: Obsolete!

KENNY: Oh shit, here we go again.

GEORGE: Reality is sometimes a little hard to digest.

WILLOW: Hey! There it is....The house...there's people there!

(Segue to FREDDIE icefishing.)

FREDDIE: *(Hoisting a bottle to his lips.)* Here's some Christmas cheer to whoever the fuck you are... *(Drinks.)* Oh yeah....

Now that's what I needed. *(Notices Northern Lights.)* What's that? Holy Shit! What's going on up there? *(Drops bottle.)* Holy Shit!

(Segue to WILLOW, GEORGE and KENNY standing outside admiring the Northern Lights)

WILLOW: Wait! Look! Look!

GEORGE: I've never seen anything like this.... It's incredible!

KENNY: It's like somebody is painting a picture across the galaxy.... Listen to me...I sound like.... I don't know who I sound like...

WILLOW: I'm going to pray.

KENNY: Willow....

GEORGE: I.... I...

(Segue back to MARY. MARY is having the baby, MAGGIE helping, having a conversation with the spirits, disembodied voices speaking in Dene helping MARY deliver the baby. The DENE MAN looks happy, but worried. Looks at Northern Lights, says something to MARY. The baby is born. They all freeze, lights dim, Northern Lights dance.)

MAHKÊSÎS: Holy Smokes! I just got a flash! Jesus Christ. *wîsahkêcâhk. nênapohš.* Glooscap. And don't forget about Mohammed, Buddha, and throw in John Lennon too. Maybe they're all the same. I mean it! I'm delirious tonight...too much dry meat, I guess...all these songs I want to play for you tonight. Yeah! This is the Fox and this is Red Skies 90.5 FM.... Normie Greenbaum and the "Spirit in the Sky".... Ho!

(Segue to WILLOW. GEORGE and KENNY arrive.)

JOE: Holy Shit! Where'd you guys come from?

MARY: *Glah na tehl...*

(They rush toward her in awe, worried, excited, talking.)

MARY: Isn't she beautiful? *(Begins to cry.)*

WILLOW: A girl! She's gorgeous, Mary!

JOE: Mary...Mary, I can't believe this...this is incredible...she's a girl.

KENNY: Congrats, man...whoever you are.

GEORGE: Mary, you don't know me. We're from the University and we brought gifts...here, take it. It's tobacco.

KENNY: Yeah, me too. I'm Kenny. We didn't know you'd be here... we were going to leave the gifts at your house... anyways, here...it's some cedar from back home in BC. I'm from the Shuswap Nation.

MARY: Oh thank you, thank you. I'm so glad you came.

WILLOW: You're Shuswap?

JOE: Well, I guess I can give you my gift. *(Goes to knapsack, produces a braid of sweetgrass and beaded baby outfit.)* Here's for our daughter.

MARY: Oh, Joe...it's a little dress...with a Dene design. How did you know?

JOE: I can dream too, you know. *(They embrace.)*

WILLOW: I guess that leaves me, Mary... here. *(Gives her deluxe pack of Pampers, they all laugh.)* It's not so traditional, but...

MAGGIE: *(Hands MARY some sage in a medicine bag.)* Here, Mary, it's sage.... For you and your beautiful daughter.

MARY: *(Begins to cry.)* You are all so beautiful. I wish I had something to give to you. *(Sees people coming in the distance.)* Look...Joe...there's people coming...who are all those people?

WILLOW: Where'd they come from?

MAGGIE: It's the Dene people, Mary, they've come to see the baby...

MARY: Joe...

JOE: We're home, Mary..... we're home....Nenidel nenidel

(The DENE MAN appears with a drum and begins to chant. MAGGIE begins the dance and the rest of the group joins in, circling MARY and JOE and the baby. Song ends and people freeze. The radio kicks in.)

MAHKÊSÎS: Hey, Hey, Hey, another great hit by The Beatles, a classic from the 70s... "Hey Jude"...to get you into the frame of mind for the season. Well, it's time for this old fox to go back to his hole, but I gotta tell you I feel ggoooood. There's a brand new feeling out there among our people...a rebirth...a sacred child in us all... *wâcistakâç...kisâkihitin*...I love you. Let's go celebrate with Red Bull and a round dance song from Red Pheasant... aaaaiiieeee.... Hoookahh...and don't forget to tune into CHIP 90.5 FM Red Skies...the heart of our nation... Ho!

(Song begins. MARY returns with traditional dress and all begin to sing and dance. MAHKÊSÎS and MAGGIE and rest of cast and audience join in and dance the night away.)

MAHKÊSÎS: ...and don't forget to look at those Northern Lights tonight...they're dancing for you.

Guide to the Pronunciation of Cree and Saulteaux Dialogue in

Mary of Patuanak

Jean L. Okimâsis and Arok Wolvengrey

In the following list of the Cree and Saulteaux vocabulary found in *Mary of Patuanak,* an approximate English pronunciation is given for each word, phrase, or sentence, along with a translation. The pronunciation is broken into syllables with primary stress indicated in FULL CAPS, while secondary stress is given in SMALL CAPS. An example of this is as follows:

maskisin . . . . *"shoe, moccasin"*
[MUSS kis SIN]

The Cree word *maskisin,* "shoe, moccasin," thus follows the same stress pattern as the English word "medicine," with primary stress on the first syllable, and a small amount of secondary stress on the final syllable.

All dialogue included in this guide is Cree, unless otherwise specified.

Act I

p. 135: **Mahkêsîs** [character's name] . . . . *"Fox"*
[MUH kay CEASE]
awâsisak . . . . *"children"*
[uh WAA sis SUCK]

p. 136: **kayâsi-nêhiyaw** . . . . *"old-time Cree(s)"*
[kuh YAAS NAY he YOW]
tâpwê . . . . *"truly"*
[taa PWAY]

p. 139: **kaskitêwiyâs** . . . . *"negro, black man"*
[KUSS kit TAY wee YAAS]
âstam . . . . *"come"*
[aas TUM]

p. 144: **wâcistakâc** . . . . *"Goodness gracious!"*
[WAATS tuh KAATS]
kôkom . . . . *"Grandma"*
[KOH koom]
mošôm . . . . *"Grandpa"*
[MOH shoom]

p 146: **kikiyâskin** . . . . *"You're lying"*
[kik KEE yaas SKIN]

p. 151: **tânisi** . . . . *"hello"*
[TAAN sih]
nêhiyawak . . . . *"Cree(s)"*
[nay HE yow WUCK]
awâsisak . . . . *"children"*
[uh WAA sis SUCK]

p. 156: **tânisi** . . . . *"hello"*
[TAAN si]

p. 160: **kôkom** . . . . *"grandma"*
[KOH koom]

p. 164: **ânîn** . . . . *"hello" (in Saulteaux)*
[AAH neen]

p. 165: **amisk** . . . . *"beaver"*
[um MISK] {repeated twice}

p. 172: **tâpwê** . . . . *"truly"*
[taa PWAY]

p. 182: **pêyak ...nîso...nisto... nêwo...** . *"one ... two ... three ... four ..."*
[pay YUCK nee SO nis TOE nay WOE]
niyânan ... (and) nikotwâsik . . . . *"five ... and six"*
[NEE yaa NUN nik CO twaa SICK]
(and a) têpakohp . . . . *"and a seven"*
[...TAY puh COPE]

p. 183: **ayênânêw ... kêkâ-... mi...tâ...taht ...** . . *"eight ... niiinnne ..."*
[uh YAY naa NAYOO kay KAA MIT taa TUHT]
mi...tâ...taht ... (a...rat...a...tat...tat!) . . . . *"tennn ..."*
[MIT taa TUHT]

p. 184: **ânîn** . . . . *"hello" (in Saulteaux)*
[AAH neen]

p. 185: **kisâkihitin** . . . . *"I love you"*
[KISS saa KIH hit TIN]
p. 188: **acâhkos** . . . . *"star"*
[UH tsaah KOOS]
p. 189: **kôna** . . . . *"snow"*
[koe NUH]
p. 192: **kihci-manitow** . . . . *"Great Spirit"*
[KIHT tsee MUN toe]
p. 196: **wîsahkêcâhk** . . . . *(Cree Trickster)*
[wee SUHK kay TSAAHK]
nênapohš . . . . *(Saulteaux Trickster)*
[NAY nuh BOOSH]
p. 198: **wâcistakâc** . . . . *"Goodness gracious!"*
[WAATS tuh KAATS]
kisâkihitin . . . . *"I love you"*
[KISS saa KIH hit TIN]

Guide to Dene Dialogue in

Mary of Patuanak

Bruce Sinclair

p. 135: **Kozigal...kozigal...s'ekwi...s'ekwi...s'ekwi degai hi nigha ha**
. . . . *"Come, come, a child is coming...a gift."*
p. 142: **s'ekwi degai hi nigha ha** . . . . *"A child is coming...a gift."*
p. 143: **Ene...seta** . . . . *"Mother, father."*
p. 152: **S'ekwi...s'ekwi degai hi nigha ha...s'ekwi degai hi nigha ha**
. . . . *"A child is coming...a gift."*
kozigal...kozigal...s'ekwi degai hi nigha ha
. . . . *"Come, come, a child is coming...a gift."*
p. 161: **Ene! Ene!** . . . . *"Mother! Mother!"*
glah na tehl...glah na tehl . . . . *"Hello, how are you? "*
seta? . . . . *"father?"*
p. 175: **Yuwe nigha, ena, thebaigha** . . . . . . *"Get away Cree man, run."*
p. 188: **Glah na tehl** . . . . *"Hello, how are you?"*
p. 191: **Sinire horelya horelya** . . . . *"All my relations."*
Kozigal...s'ekwi degai hi nigha ha
. . . . *"Come, a child is coming, a gift."*
p. 196: **Glah na tehl** . . . . *"Hello, how are you?"*

ACKNOWLEDGEMENTS

Mary of Patuanak was originally workshopped by Twenty Fifth Street Theatre of Saskatoon in May, 1994, and workshopped again by Native Earth Performing Arts in their "Weesageechak Begins to Dance" Festival of New Plays in November, 1996. *Mary of Patuanak* is yet to be produced.

Mary of Patuanak is a work in progress that has been in my subconscious and conscious psyche for many years. The concept for "Mary" came to me when I was feeling the loss of the spiritual meaning of Christmas. Her character personified the confusion and search for her spiritual self. As important was the choice of her "lost" culture, Dene or Chipewyan. I am of Métis blood, with Cree being my Indian side. Growing up in Meadow Lake, Saskatchewan, I became aware of the discrimination against the Dene by the Cree and Métis of the area. Similarly, Mary has to bear another burden, that of discrimination from the urban Indians in Saskatoon because of her Dene blood. The dream world has always fascinated me, and Mary humbly accepts her power in this incredible world. What we know about the dream world is that it is a domain with which Indian spirituality is connected in a way that perhaps only "death" will reveal.

I'd like to thank my mom, Mrs. Doreen Sinclair, for the beliefs she's instilled in me over the years. That's where Mary came from. And it's equally important to acknowledge my father, Wilfred Sinclair, who cared for us and accepted his role as a husband and parent to five wild and wonderful children. As well, heart and soul go to my wife, Lucie Joyal, whose love and caring for myself and our children, Koonis, Wasena, and Azalée truly inspire my life. Through Koonis, our first child, we were given a gift from the Creator, and this event inspired the spirit of Mary who also carried her sacred child into the world of *Mary of Patuanak.*

It is also important to note that it may seem peculiar that I linked the "mythical" Mary to the actual village of Patuanak in Northern Saskatchewan, as I had never been there and had no blood links to the Dene people. It was only recently that I learned that my biological father actually lived in Patuanak in his youth. So somehow this connection became known to me from the father I never knew, as we never really "know" who the father is of Mary's nameless child.

Thanks also to many others who have inspired and supported and listened to my stories and my humble offerings to the spirit of theatre. It is important to know that I believe this particular play *Mary of Patuanak* is still evolving and will take other forms as years go by. I hope you enjoy this version and any future offerings.

– Bruce E. Sinclair

EDITOR'S ACKNOWLEDGEMENTS

My initial thanks go to my mother, who led the way to secure funds so *Governor of the Dew: a memorial to nostalgia and love,* could be performed at the *Aboriginal Peoples and the Prairies, 2001* conference, co-sponsored by the Canadian Plains Research Center, University of Regina, and The Royal Saskatchewan Museum. Financial supporters of the performance also included: Charles Coffey, Martin Cornfield, Murray Knuttila, André Lalonde, Peter McKinnon, John McIntosh, Michael Milani, Barry & Janice Morgan, Andrew & Helen Oko, Marty Popescul, Dan Pradniuk, Donna Sigmeth, Mervyn Shaw, Allan Snell, and Lynn Starkey. SaskTel, SGI, and the Departments of Theatre and Music at the University of Regina also provided generous support.

I am grateful to Gail Bowen and Simone Hengen of the Saskatchewan Indian Federated College English department (SIFC), who taught from manuscript versions of the plays while they were being readied for publication. Thanks to Annette Dubois and Denise Kaiswatum, also of SIFC, for their support with the productions staged on campus and thanks also to Charlie Fox who made the arrangements for the theatre space, and who videotaped the plays for use in my classroom.

Thanks are also due to Bill Asikinack, Angela Weenie, Simone Hengen and Diane Zoell who got *all* of their students to the plays. A special thanks to the students themselves – some of whom were attending a live theatrical production for the first time and despite the risks, brought their entire families and friends along with them!

Jean Okimâsis and Arok Wolvengrey of the Saskatchewan Indian Federated College's Department of Indian Languages, Literatures and Linguistics, corrected and standardized the spelling of Cree words. I am grateful to them for their patience and attention to detail during the final proofing of the text, and I am also grateful to Elder Bette Spence who helped with a few Cree words. Patrick Douaud, despite returning to his family's home in Nantes, France scarcely once a year, was entrusted with the translation of the French song in *Governor of the Dew: a memorial to nostalgia and love.* My thanks to him.

Michele Sereda, Artistic Director of Curtain Razors is a valuable source of advice to me in all matters relating to the theatre, and she was my sounding board throughout the collecting, editing and teaching of these plays. Michele was professionally employed in various aspects of the productions of both *Governor of the Dew: a memorial to nostalgia and love* and *Antigone,* and for some years she has enjoyed an artistic relationship with Floyd Favel and Deanne Kasokeo.

Finally, I am grateful to my husband, Béla Szabados, for our conversations about the plays which he not only read but also discussed and attended with me.

This collection is rooted in my first exposure to the work of Floyd Favel and Deanne Kasokeo when I, along with hundreds of faculty and students, attended special performances of the plays together. This was made possible through the generosity of Globe Theatre's Artistic Director, Ruth Smillie, who saw to it that all of us from SIFC could attend the plays en masse. To Ruth we are extremely grateful. The memories – of us together in the theatre, watching the work of First Nation playwrights and directors, performed by First Nation actors – are unforgettable. Many in the audience – and we filled the house each time – had their eyes opened to the possibilities not contemplated before seeing these plays performed live – as playwrights, actors, costume designers and directors.

Governor of the Dew: a memorial to nostalgia and love, and *All My Relatives* by Floyd Favel, *Antigone* by Deanne Kasokeo, and *Mary of Patuanak* by Bruce Sinclair – all show us how the theatre can be a place where our stories, old and new, can blossom and nourish.

– HEATHER HODGSON

PHOTO: MARK PORTNOY, NEW YORK, NY

ABOUT THE EDITOR

Heather Hodgson is a freelance editor who also teaches at the Saskatchewan Indian Federated College. A contributing editor for *Books in Canada,* her editing credits also include *Seventh Generation: An Anthology of Contemporary Native Writing* and the aboriginal writing portion of *Sundog Highway*, Coteau's anthology of Saskatchewan writing. Of Plains Cree ancestry on her mother's side, she now lives and works in Regina.